Praise for
You Are Not Alone

"Dena Yohe transparently and compassio…………-centered, biblically grounded help and hope to parents in crisis. She shares what she has learned on her journey and reminds every parent that in the midst of the pain, you are not alone."

—BOB LEPINE, co-host of *FamilyLife Today*

"Parents of prodigals often wrestle with feelings of profound loneliness and alienation. In her moving account, Dena Yohe offers encouraging reminders that countless other parents have been there too. Her wise and compassionate advice is sure to comfort and uplift many hurting moms and dads."

—JIM DALY, president of Focus on the Family

"This honest book is full of Dena's wisdom, experience, and compassion. Her daughter's story has helped thousands of young people believe that no matter the circumstances they're not alone and recovery is possible. I have no doubt that Dena's perspective will do the same for parents."

—JAMIE TWORKOWSKI, founder of To Write Love on Her Arms and New York Times best-selling author of *If You Feel Too Much*

"Ms. Yohe's writing echoes in the deepest chamber of my parent-heart because she teaches me how much parent-love hurts, breaks, then heals, and—ultimately—molds us into people who can be deeply engaged in the Spirit of God. While there is no doubt that I will be using this book in my clinical counseling practice, I can also imagine that there is a hungry and vast readership that has been longing to hear from an author who understands the grit it takes to hope for a better tomorrow. She teaches us parents to 'starve our fears and feed our faith' with practical ways to grieve and respond to the difficult issues. What a vital resource!"

—MARY ELLEN MANN, LCSW, president of Last Battle
and Mann Counseling Group

"Having a child or family member struggling with things like addiction or depression can lead to so many painful days and hopeless nights. These are often places we feel so alone, but Dena and her family have been there and their words are such a gift. This is not a book of quick fixes but of practical wisdom from someone who has been down those dark roads. Dena (and Reneé) have the unique ability to offer real help with beautiful compassion, for both you and your child. This book is a wonderful resource of direction, clarity, courage, and hope. It will be a wonderful resource of not just steps in coping but also movements toward healing."

—AARON MOORE, licensed mental health counselor,
founder of Solace Counseling, and speaker for To Write
Love On Her Arms

"*You Are Not Alone* is a powerful resource written by a mom who learned how to live through her daughter's cutting, drug addiction, and depression. Her story gives Christian parents permission to be honest with their anguish, guilt, shame, and fear, but also gives them tools so they don't get lost in their child's poor choices. One of the most helpful chapters teaches how parents love their wayward child yet emotionally detach. You will learn to stop enabling, covering, or protecting, and to trust God with your child's future without forsaking your own."

—LESLIE VERNICK, LCSW, relationship coach, speaker,
and author of *The Emotionally Destructive Marriage*
and *The Emotionally Destructive Relationship*

"I've walked with Dena Yohe through much of her journey with Reneé, and she tells that story so well, so passionately, so gently, so truthfully, so hopefully. You can feel the pain she endured and the fear she survived. Gratefully she lets us in on lessons learned, where to go for help for yourself and your prodigal, and how to hold tight to your child with love and grace. If you love a prodigal, you will be so thankful for this book."

—JUDY DOUGLASS, office of the president of Cru, founder of Prayer for Prodigals and Worldwide Prodigal Prayer Day, and author of *Letters to My Children: Secrets of Success*

"The dark years of my son's heroin addiction and imprisonment changed not only his life but mine as well. In her riveting debut book, *You Are Not Alone,* Dena Yohe gives us a mother's powerful perspective on pain and suffering viewed through the lens of God's sovereignty and purpose—it is healing salve for a wounded heart."

—ALLISON BOTTKE, best-selling author of *Setting Boundaries with Your Adult Children* and the Setting Boundaries series

YOU ARE NOT ALONE

Hope for Hurting Parents of Troubled Kids

Dena Yohe

WATERBROOK

You Are Not Alone

This book is not intended to replace the advice of a trained psychological professional. Readers are advised to consult a qualified professional regarding treatment. The author and publisher specifically disclaim liability, loss, or risk, personal or otherwise, which is incurred as a consequence, directly or indirectly, of the use or application of any of the contents of this book.

Details in some anecdotes and stories have been changed to protect the identities of the persons involved.

Trade Paperback ISBN 978-1-60142-837-0
eBook ISBN 978-1-60142-838-7

Published in the United States by WaterBrook, an imprint of the Crown Publishing Group, a division of Penguin Random House LLC, New York.

WaterBrook® and its deer colophon are registered trademarks of Penguin Random House LLC.

Library of Congress Cataloging-in-Publication Data
Names: Yohe, Dena, author.
Title: You are not alone : hope for hurting parents of troubled kids / Dena Yohe.
Description: First Edition. | Colorado Springs, Colorado : WaterBrook Press, 2016. | Includes bibliographical references.
Identifiers: LCCN 2016002918 (print) | LCCN 2016012953 (ebook) | ISBN 9781601428370 (trade pbk.) | ISBN 9781601428387 (electronic)
Subjects: LCSH: Parents of children with disabilities—Religious life. | Hope—Religious aspects—Christianity.
Classification: LCC BV4596.P35 Y64 2016 (print) | LCC BV4596.P35 (ebook) | DDC 248.8/45—dc23
LC record available at http://lccn.loc.gov/2016002918

Printed in the United States of America
2016—First Edition

10 9 8 7 6 5 4 3 2 1

Special Sales
Most WaterBrook books are available at special quantity discounts when purchased in bulk by corporations, organizations, and special-interest groups. Custom imprinting or excerpting can also be done to fit special needs. For information, please e-mail specialmarketscms@penguinrandomhouse.com or call 1-800-603-7051.

To Tom, my loving, faithful, supportive husband. You believed in this book so much that you allowed yourself to be neglected many days and nights. You walked this journey by my side with incredible amounts of understanding and patience. You're my greatest cheerleader. I'm honored to share our story and what we've learned along the way. Thank you for trusting me with it.

Contents

You Will Survive

The only real tragedy is a life that ends without . . . hope.

—Nancy Guthrie, *The One Year Book of Hope*

Everyone who knew Reneé thought she was doing well. But danger lurks around every corner for recovering addicts who also struggle with mental illness and self-injury, especially in the early years of sobriety. This was my twenty-two-year-old daughter's situation. By 2009 Reneé had crisscrossed the country for three years to share her inspirational message of hope, but she had never traveled alone—until now. Reneé flew to a new city, then drove herself to a small university for a speaking engagement. That evening she, a gifted communicator, spoke to a group of students and professors. Audiences found her beauty, candor, and eloquence captivating. Amazed at how much she had overcome, many stayed after the presentation to talk with her personally.

"May I have your autograph?"

"Would you take a picture with me?"

"You're my hero. Your story saved my life."

It was both a blessing and a burden.

Since Reneé's story had gone around the world and inspired millions (via a nonprofit called To Write Love on Her Arms), this had become a common scene. But she never got used to it. For many who struggle with the same issues—addiction, cutting, mental illness, suicidal tendencies, and the sexual trauma that often accompanies a dangerous lifestyle—Reneé was a significant source of encouragement. To some, she became an idol.

In her pain-filled story, both young and old found what they needed to continue walking out their own stories: hope and courage. Hope to believe things could get better, and courage never to give up fighting for their lives.

On this night Reneé told her moving story one more time, then hung out afterward to talk with students and faculty as long as she could bear it. Unbeknownst to anyone, her recovery was unraveling. Life had been draining out without being replenished. The battle was raging and she was losing.

My mother heart was about to be crushed—again.

Shattered Peace

The phone rang in our bedroom at 3:00 a.m., piercing the peaceful silence of the night. Adrenaline pumped through my veins. Phone calls after midnight were never a good thing.

My husband, Tom, sleepily answered the phone while I struggled to catch my breath. I tried not to assume the worst, yet somehow I knew. A sense of dread welled within me.

We've been here before. I don't want to go back. I don't think I can do this again. It was brutal the first time. I'm not ready, Lord.

No one ever is.

"Hello? Reneé, is that you?" I heard Tom say.

I knew it. I wish I had been wrong. Years of experience had trained my ear to recognize the sound of distress in my husband's voice.

"What happened, honey? Where are you? What?" Panic rose in his voice.

"I can't understand you. Slow down. Please, Reneé, calm down. Take some deep breaths. You can do it. Panicking won't help. Now, what did you say?"

There was an uncomfortable pause. I hurried to Tom's side and sat beside him so I could hear both sides of the conversation.

"I'm scared, Daddy." *If she's afraid, it must be bad,* I thought.

"What are you afraid of, honey?" he asked calmly.

"I can't get the bleeding to stop!"

Oh, God, no. I covered my mouth to keep from screaming.

"And I've been drinking." Crying like a baby, she confessed, "Oh, Daddy, I took too many pills."

Letting out a groan, I doubled over. I felt as if I were sobbing deep in my gut, though nothing audible came out of my mouth. Tom began to pace.

"How many pills did you take, Reneé?"

She whimpered, "I don't know! I don't know!"

"Where are you?" he asked, on the verge of tears.

"I'm in my hotel room. I'm on the floor in the bathroom. I'm getting sleepy and there's so much blood." She sounded groggy. "I don't know what to do!"

Nausea swept over me. I envisioned blood dripping from scarred arms onto pristine tiles.

Then, in a voice filled with remorse, she said, "Oh, Daddy, I feel so guilty. I don't want to disappoint all those people who look up to me."

"Oh, Reneé, I know you don't," Tom reassured. "I understand. It's really, really hard. I'm so sorry, honey."

Don't worry about them right now. Your life is in danger!

As I listened, salty tears streamed down my cheeks. *Her heart is so beautiful. How can she be so broken?*

Tom said, "But listen to me. No one expected you to be perfect."

Not in the beginning, but maybe I had started to. The realization jolted me.

Reneé stammered an unintelligible response.

Tom continued, "You made a mistake, but you're going to get back up and begin again. You're going to be okay. It won't be easy, but you can do it."

Yes. Yes. With God's help, you can. Hearing the confidence in my husband's voice increased mine. All I could hear from the receiver was weeping.

"You've come so far, Reneé. Remember, the only way you can fail is to give up."

"I won't give up, Daddy. I won't."

I wanted to believe her with all my heart.

"Okay, now you've got to listen to me closely and do exactly what I tell you. Don't hang up, but put your cell phone down. Grab some towels and wrap up your arms. Then go find the hotel phone in your room and call the front desk. Tell them it's an emergency. Then come right back to your phone in the bathroom. I'll be waiting here for you. Go do it right now."

Oh, my precious princess, hurry back to your phone. Don't go too far away. Daddy and I will be waiting for you.

I rocked back and forth as I sat on the side of our bed in the darkness, shaking and praying.

We waited. Not knowing how severe her wounds were or how much danger she was in was pure torture.

Finally, we heard her weak voice on the phone again. Tom and I let out a collective sigh of relief. Thank God. Help was on the way.

"Good job, sweetheart. I'll stay here with you and keep talking until help arrives. I know you're scared. I understand how much you hate hospitals and psych wards, but your life may be at stake."

Please let them get there in time. We didn't even know the name of the hotel or we would have called for help ourselves. *I beg You, God, please save my child.*

The next words I heard from Reneé stunned me. "Are you mad at me, Daddy? I didn't mean to hurt you and Mom like this."

Dear God, help me.

Tom shook his head as he almost shouted, emphasizing each word, "Oh, no, Reneé! *No.* We're not mad. We hurt for you. It breaks our hearts to see you in so much pain. We love you. We'll always be here for you!"

Her next question broke me wide open. "Can you forgive me? Can you and Mom ever forgive me?"

Falling to his knees, Tom choked, "Yes, of course we forgive you, Reneé. You don't *ever* have to wonder about that. We love you no matter what. We've always told you there's nothing you could do that would make us love you any more or any less. Nothing will ever change that. Nothing."

WHERE IT ALL BEGAN

Ten years before, I noticed the early warning signs of trouble, but I didn't know what they meant—or I didn't want to know. When Reneé was twelve she cut herself the first time and began to show symptoms of depression.

Little did I know she had a problem that would become serious and life threatening.

Or where this journey would lead.

Or how much pain it would bring.

I never could have imagined my daughter's gradual, bumpy recovery from substance abuse and other life-altering issues. I never dreamed her story would be the beginning of an international nonprofit called To Write Love on Her Arms (TWLOHA.com), bringing hope to millions of hurting men and women all over the world.

Little did I know how her life would change mine.

But this is not Reneé's story. That is for her to tell. This is my story—my perspective as a mother who learned to cope with deep pain, a mom who learned to let go of broken dreams and discover new ones.

I'm not the only one. Countless parents struggle as I have—and maybe you have too. We wrestle with the same feelings of denial, shock, disappointment, hurt, anger, fear, and loss. Most of all, we don't want anyone to know. We tend to suffer alone. Lacking support and feeling devoid of hope, we struggle in isolation. And our heartache intensifies.

LESSENING THE HEARTACHE

Let's pause for a moment. I want to clarify that this is not a how-to-change-or-fix-your-child book. I have no strategies for guaranteed success. No tips to avoid trouble. I can't tell you how to do that.

But, parent, you are my focus. Lending you a hand as you try to cope with what might be the most excruciating experiences of your life is the whole point. My goal is to share what helped me, what got me through my darkest days, not knowing how the future would unfold.

Friend, fellow parent, when we're willing to be honest, to share our pain with other hurting parents and hear others' stories, something unexpected happens. A mysterious exchange takes place. Our discouragement lessens and we find the strength we lacked. We let go of despair and unearth fresh comfort, even community. We find the courage to press on.

And then, at last, we realize we aren't alone. We can make it—together. If I'm able to continue my journey without knowing how it will end, then maybe you can too. I may not know the future for my child, but I know Who holds it. I can trust God with all my tomorrows and all of Reneé's. With His help, you and I can find strength and comfort to carry us through our worst times.

Again, I can't tell you how to keep your child from making mistakes. But I can encourage and equip you with facts, tools, and resources. I can show you—weary, worn-out Mom or Dad—you can survive this nightmare. Not only that, I'm confident that one day, somehow, you can thrive again.

"Impossible," you say. "How can you make such a ludicrous statement?" I can tell you how: personal experience, from the core of my belief and the foundation of my hope, based on the words of Jesus, "With man this is impossible, but with God all things are possible" (Matthew 19:26). These are the very things I want to unpack in the chapters that follow.

It's my prayer that in the pages ahead you'll find new hope and come to believe you can thrive again. I'll share my honest journey, including mistakes made, eye-opening discoveries, and ways to cope that you might not have thought of. You'll read about the truths God showed me and the steps I took that made all the difference. You'll find resources and hear from experts and from fellow parents on a similar path. Renee will also offer her insights where appropriate, providing a once-troubled child's viewpoint. They're things she wants you to know. I wish I had known them years ago. And each chapter will end with scriptures that helped me. I hope they'll help you too.

Scripture That Helps

Lean on, trust in, and be confident in the Lord with all your heart and mind and do not rely on your own insight or understanding. In all your ways know, recognize, and acknowledge Him, and He will direct and make straight and plain your paths. (Proverbs 3:5–6, AMPC)

2

An Unexpected Journey

An expectation is a premeditated resentment.

—Al-Anon

When our issues with Reneé began, I thought back to when I first became a mother. At the seasoned age of thirty I had felt ready to be a mom. But as Reneé grew up, it became more of a challenge than I could have imagined—much more. This was not how I imagined my parenting journey would go. How could being a mom be so painful? It was bewildering.

Maybe you relate. In the beginning I was full of starry-eyed goals, high hopes, and beautiful dreams. *Being a mother is going to be the best part of my life,* I thought. Every day would be a delightful, making-wonderful-memories experience, right? Sure, we would encounter some bumps along the way. But with plenty of love, biblical wisdom, healthy boundaries, reasonable consequences, gentle-but-firm teaching, and lots of prayer, we'd all be fine. We'd end up a close, affectionate family who celebrated one another's successes, supported one another in our hard times, enjoyed being together, were able to trust one another at all times, and helped one another in ways that mattered. Right?

Are you laughing? Who thinks things will be good all the time while raising children? I did, for one.

What a surprise I was in for. My ideals were more fantasy than reality, especially with our middle child, Reneé. Michael, my firstborn, was four years older, and April was two years younger than Reneé. While they had a few bumps in the road growing up, both were easy to raise. They were peacemakers and eager to please, responsive to boundaries and wonderfully obedient. But with Reneé there would be plenty of frustrations and unfulfilled expectations. There would be enough hurt to fill an entire bookshelf. In our first troubled days of her toddlerhood, we knew challenging years were ahead. By the time she was twelve, we began to experience more problems. I thought, *These things only happen to other people. Not to me. Not to my child. I'm a good mother. Haven't I done it all right?*

When Reneé's problems refused to be easily or quickly resolved, finally I had to admit that the experience was going to affect me for the rest of my life. I didn't like that. But I've come to accept it.

It's taken more than ten years to become emotionally and spiritually healthy. I'm still working on it. It's a slow process.

Maybe you know exactly what I'm talking about. Has parenting taken you on an unexpected journey with more anguish than you thought possible? If so, hang on. I've learned some things that will help you endure and, as I mentioned in chapter 1, even thrive despite the pain you're in. And I'm ready to share them with you.

THE BEAUTY OF ACCEPTANCE

How well people cope with trials and troubles—anything outside of their control—depends on how well they accept life's disappointments. *Merriam-Webster* defines *accept* as "to agree to receive whether willingly or reluctantly; to put up with (something painful or difficult)" In my opinion, the last phrase nails it.

Initially I was not willing to deal with the scenario we faced. Feelings of resentment fought against my ability to accept my situation. I thought

I'd been given a raw deal. How many times did I want to shout, "It's not fair!"? Have you said this too? After all, against our will, we were thrown into a gigantic mess by the choices and behaviors of our children. Because of my daughter's struggles, I found myself in a foreign environment I knew nothing about: a world of addiction, rehab programs, self-injury, mental illness, and more. I had no idea what to do for her or for me. As a parent, I thought I was supposed to know how to help her and keep her safe. Feeling helpless was so unexpected. It felt terrible.

In my desperation I sought ways to relieve the stress, even a little bit, and stumbled across some good tools. You can try these yourself and see if they help you accept your child's situation and energize you for coping.

Get Educated

One way I found the willingness to tolerate this utterly difficult and most unpleasant situation with my daughter was to educate myself on her issues. I read everything I could get my hands on to learn about Reneé's substance abuse, self-harm, and so forth.

Ignorance was my downfall. In an attempt to change that, I attended a class to understand more about mental health issues. Learning about the problems she struggled with equipped me to face reality better. The Internet, books, experienced parents, counselors, and support groups like Al-Anon were also a huge help. Becoming informed empowered me, lowered my stress, lessened my fears, and increased my understanding of what was happening. I grew stronger and felt more capable when I faced difficult situations.

I recommend that you, too, empower yourself through education on the issues. Because I know how overwhelming this can be, I've included a reading and resources list at the back of the book as a place to begin.

Adjust Your Expectations

Living through my worst nightmares changed me. Quite honestly, I'll never be the same. I have to accept that. If I can't, then I'm setting myself up for bigger problems. I had to adjust my expectations of God, myself, my children, my family, my friends, and life in general. I adjusted by identifying my expectations and hopes and lowering them. Instead of expecting God to keep bad things from happening to my daughter, I learned to trust Him with what I couldn't understand. Instead of expecting myself to be the perfect mom, I accepted that I wasn't, but that was okay. I knew I was doing the best I could. Instead of expecting my children to embrace my beliefs or do what I wanted (like get a college degree), I accepted that they were free to make their own choices. My goals and values couldn't be forced on them. Instead of expecting my husband or my friends to satisfy my longings in our relationships and understand my needs, I accepted that no human being could fully do that. They did their best, but we all let each other down at times. No one but God is perfect. Only He could satisfy me. And instead of expecting life to be fair, I accepted that sometimes it isn't. That's how things are. But God is good, and He uses all things to accomplish His purposes. Doing these things relieved a lot of pressure and lowered my stress level.

How did I reform my expectations? I listened to the wisdom of recovering addicts, other moms and dads with struggling kids, various professionals, and people living well with mental illness. I learned so much from them. I met many of them at conferences and in classes and recovery support groups for hurting parents. I read some of their stories in books that were recommended and listened to a great radio program called *New Life Live* led by several counselors and psychologists.

I also left guilt, embarrassment, and shame at the door.

I abandoned guilt when I stopped blaming myself and finally accepted the truth that my daughter's problems weren't my fault. At one of the first Al-Anon meetings I attended, the leader told us we needed to refuse this emotion. He said it was wasted energy and that our loved ones made their own choices, thus it didn't make any difference how good or bad of a parent we had been. Nothing we did or didn't do was a sufficient excuse for their destructive choices. Mental health issues aren't our fault, either. We didn't choose that for them. Heredity is beyond our control. It is what it is, as a dear friend of mine likes to say. Wallowing in guilt only makes us worse off. It helps no one.

I abandoned embarrassment when I met more and more parents—great parents, godly parents, much-better-than-I parents—in the same boat (or worse) and realized I wasn't the only one. When I saw how they were willing to be honest with what they were going through, it encouraged me to do the same. Setting aside my pride allowed me to find courage and strength from their example. If they could be vulnerable, then so could I. Then my daughter's story became very public, and this helped. There was no need to hide anymore. Everything was out in the open. It turned out to be a blessing in disguise.

I abandoned shame when I remembered that God is the perfect parent to billions of wayward, troubled sons and daughters who are disobedient, disrespectful, disloyal, and disappointing—beginning with His first two (Adam and Eve), who completely broke His heart and shattered His dreams. I'm in good company. What is there to be ashamed of anymore?

I encourage you to join me. It's humbling, yes, but abandoning guilt, embarrassment, and shame facilitates moving forward in a healthy way.

Adjust Your Mind-Set

Another way I found acceptance was to think of this experience as a race. Distance runners are willing to do whatever it takes to cross the finish line. They know it will demand every ounce of courage, strength, and endurance they've got. They consent to the process. It may be extremely difficult, but they accept the challenge. As a parent, can you accept the challenge before you? You've probably heard the phrase, "This isn't a sprint; it's a marathon." There's a lot of truth to that. I didn't understand this in the beginning. That's another adjustment I made: realizing this journey might not be over quickly. How I hoped it would, but lowering expectations helped me to be more patient with the process, especially when we experienced setbacks. After all, most of us don't change overnight, do we? I don't. It takes time, effort, falling down, and getting up—repeatedly.

Here are some healthy mind-sets I adopted. I encourage you to embrace them:

- I can walk this path only one day at a time. It can't be rushed.
- I must not dwell on the past or regret it. It can't be changed.
- I must not live in fear or dread of the future. It can't be controlled.

I know that if I am able to do this, you can too.

It still breaks my heart that we didn't know about Reneé's private struggles when they first started, when she was a young child. She was a preteen when they became noticeable. We would've gotten her help sooner instead of waiting until she was seventeen, when more serious problems had developed. Would it have made a difference? No one knows. Would it have altered some of our decisions? Maybe. But we can't redo the past. We have to let go of regrets.

We have to accept what we can't change. We have to forgive ourselves and move forward, not dreading the future. We can't change that, either. But God is in the past, the present, and the future. We can leave it all with Him.

TRUTH IS YOUR FRIEND

There are three things I wish I had learned sooner in my parenting marathon. Once I heard them at a conference for hurting parents, they were like medicine for my sickened heart. I want you to hear them sooner rather than later.

1. **You are not alone.** We need to repeat these words to ourselves until we believe them. This desperate situation isn't happening just to you and your family. You're in good company! There are thousands, if not millions, of parents all over the world who suffer with children in turmoil.

2. **You are not a bad parent.** Although you weren't and aren't perfect, no one is—and that's not your fault. Children have free will to make their own choices. Some of their troubles are genetic, such as mental illness or the propensity for alcoholism.

3. **You are going to be okay.** You will get through this. You can learn to let go and be at peace with unthinkable circumstances. You can! Joy will return, even if your child never does. You can find new purpose, new dreams and goals, and enjoy life again.

Let out a deep sigh of relief. *Whew.* These three statements might be the best things you've heard in a long time. Take a minute right now to write them on an index card or a piece of paper. Put it someplace where you'll see it often.

GET SOME COMMUNITY

As a hurting parent, you may be asking, "What did I do wrong? How could God let this happen? How will I survive? Where can I find help? Is there any hope?" Providing answers to these questions is the heart of this book.

Remember, you're in a long-distance run. You may have no clue what mile you're on. At times you think you catch a glimpse of the finish line just around the next corner, but it's elusive. You can't quite get there.

If you're running alone, I have a suggestion. *Don't.*

Remember Dorothy in *The Wizard of Oz*? She found herself on an unexpected journey with no one except her dog. Then she made a few new friends who were all looking for solutions to their needs. What did they do? They locked arms as they traveled the yellow brick road and encountered its hazards together. As a group, they pressed on toward the Emerald City.

Alone, they were overwhelmed; they succumbed to their fears and obstacles. But when they came together, they found the courage and strength they needed to keep going. They became a healing community, sharing common pain and goals.

In community we can find the encouragement we need to finish the race by doing the hard things we could never attempt on our own: get up to speed on the issues our children are facing, modify our expectations, alter our mind-sets, grasp vital truths about who we are, and find some fellow parents to travel with. Please reach out for help from others who understand. Don't run this marathon alone. Side by side we can finish our race. If I can keep running, then you can too, even if it's uphill all the way.

We can do it—together.

Scripture That Helps

Let us run with perseverance the race marked out for us, fixing our eyes on Jesus. (Hebrews 12:1–2)

The LORD is my shepherd, I lack nothing. He makes me lie down in green pastures, he leads me beside quiet waters, he refreshes my soul. He guides me along the right paths for his name's sake. Even though I walk through the darkest valley, I will fear no evil, for you are with me; your rod and your staff, they comfort me. . . . Surely your goodness and love will follow me all the days of my life, and I will dwell in the house of the LORD forever. (Psalm 23:1–4, 6)

3

Disappointment

No one is exempt from tragedy or disappointment—God himself was not exempt. Jesus offered no immunity, no way *out* of the unfairness, but rather a way *through* it to the other side.

—Philip Yancey, *Disappointment with God*

In an attempt to understand Reneé's behaviors, many have asked about her early years.

"What was her childhood like?"

"How would you describe your parenting style?"

"What do you think you did wrong?"

Ouch. That hurt, but I wondered too.

As loving, conscientious parents, Tom and I wanted to find an explanation for why things turned out the way they did. Dealing with well-meaning questions was difficult because we guessed what some people were thinking—and maybe they were right.

What in the world did you do to her?

Was there hidden dysfunction in your home?

Did you have too many rules? Too few?

Did you overindulge, deprive, or abuse your daughter?

What kind of trauma did she experience in her childhood? There must have been something.

All of their unspoken questions implied guilt and blame. *It had to be something we did—or didn't do.* Was that true? When people start offering hurtful explanations for your child's problems, implying it's somehow your fault, give yourself permission to end the conversation and walk away. Don't argue with them or waste your time and energy defending yourself. I remember when a relative asked us what we thought we did wrong that Reneé turned out like she did. "Didn't you discipline her enough?" Boy, that stung.

Simply say something like the following: "It was nice seeing you today, but I really have to leave now." "Look at the time! I've got to get going." "Thank you for sharing your thoughts. I'll keep them in mind." Remind yourself that they haven't walked in your shoes, so they really can't understand. They mean well, but they don't have any idea how their comments affect you.

When our children were young, we wanted to know how other parents raised great kids. We wanted to be sure we did all the right things. After all, we took parenting very seriously. Children didn't come easily for us.

DREAMS OF BECOMING A MOM

In my late twenties, having been married several years, I began to long for a child. One of the things that attracted me to Tom was knowing he'd be a great dad. Difficulties conceiving, however, made us wonder if we'd be able to have children. I went through a wide range of emotions and attitudes, not to mention some unfair assessments of God's goodness.

After a long year of trying, Tom said, "Honey, maybe we should consider adoption."

"I don't want to think about that—not yet. But I'm open to the idea if I can't get pregnant. Let's wait a little longer and see what happens, okay?"

After several more months of trying, we struggled with despair and discouragement. We talked with wise friends, considered seeing a specialist (but never did), spent time in prayer, read books about prayer, and read the Bible for encouragement as we wrestled with God. One day I finally relinquished to Him my desires to have a child.

Lord, it's hard, but I'm willing to let go of what I want. I'm willing to accept whatever You give. May Your will be done. That's all I want. You really are enough for me.

I surrendered. I let go of my disappointment and trusted God with the outcome.

To my surprise and delight, one month later I was expecting. We were ecstatic. But at eighteen weeks, our joy turned to sorrow when I had a miscarriage. Grief-stricken, I cried out to God, *Why did You let my baby die? Where are You?*

After six months of grieving, we were ready to try again. *I'm ready, but I'm scared, Lord,* I told Him. *I'm not sure what You have for me, but I'll keep trusting.* After another long year of trying and waiting, I was pregnant again. Frightened, I wondered, *What if we lose this baby too? If it happened once, it can happen again.*

Tests finally confirmed all was well. At last, we could begin to let ourselves get excited. We relaxed into preparing for a new phase of life: parenthood.

My dream was to be the best mom I could be. I pictured myself showering my children with love and attention, playing with them, making frequent trips to the library, reading books together, having their friends over, baking their favorite goodies, creating fun and memorable experiences. I imagined being fully present in their lives and having no regrets.

Before we knew it, our baby arrived. Elated, I thought, *It's unbelievable. I'm a mommy.* Our son, Michael, was born on my thirtieth birthday. I had prayed to have a child by the time I was thirty, but I didn't mean on that exact birthday. *God, You sure have a sense of humor.*

You know the indescribable joy of holding your firstborn. I would tell my friends, "Being a mom is more wonderful than I ever thought possible." Michael's sweet personality and compliant nature made the job pretty easy for this first-time mother.

At the time, Tom was the pastor of a small, rural church in western Pennsylvania. Since his salary was enough to make ends meet, I had the freedom to be a stay-at-home mom. I didn't want to miss anything as our little boy grew up. This was in the early eighties, when women's roles were shifting. To have value and worth, society said, women needed careers—mothers included. Television commercials reminded us we could have it all, but I didn't care. Having been a social worker, I wanted now to be a full-time wife and mom, giving focused love and attention to my husband and son. This would provide all the value and worth I needed.

Life was good.

"Who Are You Mad At?"

After Michael's second birthday, we began to think about having another baby. We wanted to expand our happy little family. "Being parents is so easy and fun," we reasoned, "let's have another child."

Conception was much easier this time; however, another midterm miscarriage left me crushed with sadness. A few months later I confided to Tom, "What's going on with me? Everything's fine, yet I'm irritable and on edge. The smallest thing makes me cry. I've never felt like this before. Something must be wrong."

"Honey, maybe you should see a counselor. If you want me to, I'll make an appointment for you."

"You really think I need to see a counselor?" *Is it that bad?*

"It can't hurt, right?"

I guess. "Well, I don't know what else to do. I don't like feeling this way."

Asking a lot of *why* questions—the kind no human can answer—

wasn't helping, and I had plenty of them. *If God is really all-powerful and loving, then why did He let this happen? Is He punishing us? Why does He let bad things happen to good people?*[1]

The counselor, Earl, turned out to be a wise man. God used him to help me make a significant discovery I would need later in my journey as a parent. I shuffled into Earl's office for the first time on a cold, dreary afternoon. Embarrassed and apprehensive, I insisted Tom come along.

After some initial friendly conversation, during which I told Earl about my recent miscarriage, commenting that I'd lost my first child the same way, he gently said, "Dena, I believe you're still grieving the loss of your first baby. This recent miscarriage hit you harder because you never fully grieved the first one. You've suffered two major losses. I'm pretty sure you're suffering from a mild case of depression. This is common after a miscarriage. They're significant events our culture doesn't recognize or address very well."

No one had spoken to me like this about my miscarriages. Not my doctor. Not anyone. A few sympathetic, older women told me they had had miscarriages too, and one compassionate friend empathized, but in general, most people didn't say much. Their silence hurt deeply and persuaded me to hide my feelings.

Surprised and relieved by Earl's comments, I said, "Depressed? Really? That's what's wrong with me? I had no idea."

"Dena," he continued, "please don't be offended, but I'd like to ask you a question."

"Well, okay."

"Who are you mad at?"

Somewhat startled and a little insulted, I replied, "What? I'm not mad at anyone."

He nodded with understanding. "I know you're a really nice person. You probably think you never get mad at anybody."

That's right, I don't.

"So take your time and think about it for a few minutes."

Earl's office was small. He sat behind a well-worn, dark wood desk while Tom and I were seated across from him in padded chairs that had seen better days. The smell of musty, old books filled the air. Overflowing bookshelves lined the walls. While I fidgeted uncomfortably in my chair, I pondered his soul-searching question. *Is it possible? Am I angry?* Then all at once it hit me. *Uh-oh, I am. I'm mad—at God.*

Remarkable. All it took to open my eyes was a simple question. I mumbled reluctantly, "Um, I didn't realize it before, but I think I actually am mad—at God. Isn't it wrong for a Christian to feel that way? I'm confused."

God might not like it if He knew what I was thinking and feeling, I thought. Oops! What was I saying? He's God. Nothing escapes Him.

Are you angry at anyone? Do you think you could be mad at God? Do you need to talk to Him about it? Why not pause here and take a few minutes to do that right now or make time when it's better for you. It could really help.

"God knows exactly how you feel, Dena," Earl responded. "It's okay to be mad at Him. He understands. It's all right. He's big enough to take it. And He doesn't love you any less." Whew. What a relief.

He continued, "Did you know that repressed anger can turn into depression?" *No. I didn't.* "It's in our best interest to be completely honest with God. We need to, for the sake of our emotional health. He wants us to tell Him everything, all the time—good and bad. We need to get in the habit. If we don't let out our negative emotions, if we hold them in, we end up hurting ourselves and those who love us."

I pondered his words. "I see what you're saying. That makes perfect sense. I had no idea I was angry. I was so disappointed with God that I buried my feelings, thinking they were wrong."

The counselor's words were healing oil for my soul. Not giving myself permission to express anger caused me to become stuck in my grief. Learning to be honest, with myself and with God, turned out to be significant for my healing, both this day and in my future.

Earl sent me home with an assignment called The Chair (see also "The Chair Exercise" in the back of this book):

Go to a quiet, private place when you have a block of unhurried time. Sit in a comfortable chair with another chair across from you or in front of a couch. Take a few moments to be still and quiet your thoughts. Take three slow, deep, cleansing breaths in through your nose and out through your mouth. Pretend God is in the chair across from you. Now, tell Him everything you've been holding inside. Say it out loud—include questions. Let your feelings go without censorship. Cuss and yell if you need to. Pound your fist. Stomp your feet. When you've expressed everything you want to say, close your eyes and ask God what He wants to say back to you. Wait patiently. Listen closely. Don't rush.

"I know it sounds weird, but try it. You may be surprised. Be sure to have pen and paper nearby to record what you sense God says. You don't want to forget."

How powerful this exercise turned out to be! God spoke to my heart every time, not audibly, but in my spirit, reassuring me of His love and care. Words of compassion and empathy flooded my mind. *I understand, My child. I know. It's okay. I still love you.*

During those times my heavenly Father reminded me that there was nothing wrong with being angry. How freeing to discover it was okay to be mad—even at Him.

Reading through the psalms brought a welcome reminder that God's Word covered every emotion—including anger. In Psalm 73 I read, "When my heart was grieved and my spirit embittered, I was senseless and ignorant; I was a brute beast before you" (verses 21–22). God never reprimanded the author for his honesty. He listened to him and accepted him. Then the man praised God, saying, "Yet I am always with you; you hold me by my right hand. You guide me with your counsel" (verses 23–24). He did the same for me.

The Chair Exercise dramatically facilitated my inner healing. It helped me accept disappointment and loss. In the future, when facing greater ones with Reneé, I would use it again. Please try it. You might be surprised how much it can help you with your inner healing.

SECRET, SILENT PAIN MAKES US SICK

Some say that time heals all wounds. Hogwash. Time never healed anyone's wounds. Untreated, hidden, and ignored, wounds fester and worsen. Al-Anon leaders are right when they say, "Secrets make us sick." God used my counselor to help me make a significant discovery: when we face our pain and stop stuffing it; when we let out repressed hurt, anger, and disappointment; when we give ourselves permission to be honest, ask hard questions, and replace the lies we've believed with truth, we can find relief and healing. Secrets—and disappointments—can't make us sick anymore.

In our heads we know that God is God and we are not. We really do believe He's in control over all things—even our mess. He doesn't owe us an explanation for the mysteries of this world. "Can you fathom the mysteries of God?" (Job 11:7). No, we can't. But if we're really honest, we might think we've become entitled. Down deep in our hearts we thought we were exempt from bad things happening to us or to one of our children. We thought we had a free pass from that kind of suffering. I did. "For he makes his sun rise on the evil and on the good, and sends rain on the just and on the unjust" (Matthew 5:45, ESV). It's as though our heads and our hearts are at war. We know these truths, but do we really believe them? Bottom line, we don't always know why God allows what He does, nor do we know why He doesn't always intervene to rescue us from the situations we're in.

But we can trust in His "everlasting love" (Jeremiah 31:3). We can lean on His sovereignty; He is "the blessed and only Ruler, the King of kings and Lord of lords" (1 Timothy 6:15). We can rest in His care. We can come to accept unanswered questions and disappointments. Can you?

If we can do these things, then we can know joy and peace no matter what we encounter in life. When disappointments cripple and break us, we can make peace with those unsolved problems because we know God's unchanging character. We can walk through our darkest days with courage and hope even though we don't know how things will end. God knows and He's in our storms with us. Somehow, some way, we will be okay.

Scripture That Helps

In this world you will have trouble. But take heart!
I have overcome the world. (John 16:33)

4

Denial

I don't believe my son would ever do that. I'd know if
there was a problem. Besides, he's a good boy. Sure, he
drinks sometimes with his friends, but he wouldn't smoke
pot or use harder drugs. We didn't raise him that way. And
he certainly wouldn't ever steal from us. He'd never . . .

—A Mom

Four years after Michael's birth, Tom had the privilege of cutting
Reneé's umbilical cord as his eyes brimmed with tears. At the end of
the birthing table, my doctor held up our brand-new baby girl. With her
not-yet-cleaned-up little body in his big, blue-gloved hands, he asked,
"Have you chosen a name for her yet?"

"Yes, we have. Reneé Ann," I announced, bursting with joy.

"Beautiful. Dena, Tom, would you mind if I prayed for Reneé right
now?"

"Please do! We'd love that."

Since he was one of my regular doctors, we knew he shared our faith.
"God, we thank You for bringing Reneé Ann into the world today. I ask
for Your hand of blessing on her life. Watch over her as she grows up.
Help Tom and Dena be the best parents they can be. Give them the wisdom and strength they're going to need to raise her. Only You know the
challenges she'll face. May she come to know You and love You with all

her heart. May Your will be done in her life. In the name of Jesus, the Author of Life, amen."

Yes, Lord, yes.

Once the medical team checked her out and cleaned her up, the nurse placed Reneé in her daddy's arms. He lovingly lowered her into a specially prepared warm bath, which was positioned for me to watch from the birthing bed. Articles we'd read made it sound like a peaceful, soothing experience. But as soon as Tom submerged our newborn into the warm water we heard "Waaaaaaa!" Ear-piercing wails filled the air.

What is this? She isn't supposed to scream. None of the videos we'd watched showed a baby in distress. The bath was meant to be calming, not upsetting.

This was the first indication of what was to come. This was the first time denial began to rage.

THE REFUGE OF MANY HURTING PARENTS

When we chose the name Reneé, we had no idea how much she would need to experience its meaning: "reborn, to rise again."[2]

As people of Christian faith, we hoped one day our children would choose to embrace this faith and make it their own, that they would experience a spiritual rebirth, a regeneration of their spirits, the eternal part of their being. Of course, this would be their choice, their own decision to make when they were old enough to understand.

Some children don't care for their names, but Reneé always liked hers. It suited her well. All through school she never had a friend or classmate with the same name. But she never liked her middle name. Around age eight, she looked at me with her big green eyes and asked in disgust, "Mom, why did you pick Ann for my middle name? It's so plain and boring! It doesn't fit me at all." It didn't. Over time she showed us there was nothing plain or ordinary about her.

Being Reneé's mom didn't end up being anything like I thought it would be either. I denied that for a long time. And please don't misunderstand. There have been countless wonderful times, moments of great celebration to be remembered forever. But there have also been too many horrific times to count, too many moments of anguish never to be forgotten.

When she was in elementary school, we had noticed Reneé's strong, unusual reactions to sounds and smells, the texture of certain foods in her mouth, the feel of certain materials on her skin, and so on. They intensified during adolescence. *Why is she acting like this? Why is she so sensitive and difficult?* I wondered. How could we account for her reactions besides stubbornness? How else could we explain her behaviors? Nothing could be wrong, not with our child.

Tom and I did our best. We raised her the same way we did her brother and her sister. We did all we could to provide a loving, nurturing, emotionally healthy environment with a strong spiritual foundation. Still, Reneé had a secret inner world of darkness, confusion, and turmoil. And she didn't want to face these things either; she managed to keep the monsters of depression, self-hatred, and anxiety well hidden. I don't know how she did it. But they refused to remain buried. With the onset of Reneé's adolescence, the monsters began to slip out.

Denial set in again when Reneé cut herself the first time at the age of twelve. *Isn't this just another one of her temper tantrums?* I thought. But mental health counselor Robin Nicolas countered this assumption: "Contrary to popular belief, people who self-harm are not doing so to get attention. In fact, most of those who cut or harm themselves do not want others to know. They carry a sense of shame and guilt not a sense of pride. When they show their scars or marks to others it is a plea for help not a cry for attention."[3]

Cutting is a complex behavior that can become a chronic, progressive addiction. Frequently misunderstood, cutting should never be ignored. We couldn't ignore the incident itself, but we could avoid and deny it as

Reneé: What a Diagnosis Can Mean for Your Child

Looking back, I don't believe I thought there was anything necessarily wrong with me in the beginning. I thought my struggle was just a part of life, that everyone experienced these things. Spiritual attacks seemed like a natural response to my decision to love God. One of the earliest moments that I felt a separation between me and "normal" was when I cut the first time. I was shocked and mortified and ashamed. I knew something was wrong, but it was too much, too big for me to deal with. I was just as much in denial about the problem as my parents were.

I just wanted it to go away, I didn't want to talk about it, and I was grateful that we didn't. It wasn't until years later, with the help of a counselor, that I realized how unhealthy that was. That perhaps the silence was invalidating and dismissive, that by not speaking about it we allowed lies to do all of the talking. Some of those lies were that I needed to handle hard things on my own; that my pain was too much and would hurt the people I loved; that no one would know what to do with it anyway. I didn't want to hurt anyone by showing them my struggles, and I didn't want to feel it either.

I wouldn't have admitted it then, and it's still hard to say, but when my parents didn't talk about the cutting after the incident, I think I subconsciously felt unloved. Not as a whole, but in that moment. Later I came to understand it wasn't that they didn't love me when I was hurting or struggling, but they didn't know how to. Who can blame them for that? We don't always know how to best love the people around us when they're grieving or their pain takes forms that are foreign to us.

It's easier to look back and say, "Well, my parents should've done this or that." I guess the most important thing would've been for us to talk about what was going on when I first started cutting. To ask questions and search for the answers they didn't have. Providing a safe space for me to process and heal with a counselor if I wasn't able or comfortable enough to share with my parents may have been a great gift for all of us.

I had all the sensitivity symptoms my mom mentioned plus I couldn't stand a gentle touch. I used to wonder why something like a soft hug from my own parents would make me feel so angry. Didn't I love them? Was something wrong with me?

Then I was diagnosed with sensory processing disorder and read a book about it. I learned that sensitivity to certain types of touch was a part of it. I was so relieved to know there was an explanation for what I had been feeling and that I wasn't rejecting their love when their touch aggravated me. I learned how to communicate my needs to my parents, that strong hugs and firm touch are calming to me. It was a simple adjustment that made a huge difference in my relationship with my family and others. The diagnosis was such a relief. I understand myself so much better now! Parents, I encourage you to come out of denial that your child has a problem. As hard as it is to admit, please take them to a professional as soon as you realize something might be wrong. That's the one thing I wish my parents had done differently: gotten me help sooner. You can't force your child to cooperate with a counselor, but at least you can provide them with the opportunity. Then it's up to them what they do with it. At least you tried.

much as possible. It would be years before we could talk about the cutting with her. We presented the idea of seeing a counselor as more of a threat or punishment than as a positive means of help. That's embarrassing to admit. Shocked and mystified, we just wanted the cutting—and the reasons behind it—to go away. And it did for a while, until it resurfaced with greater intensity after Reneé's sixteenth birthday. Still, admitting there might be something wrong was too hard.

With no knowledge about self-injury, we had no idea how to respond. We didn't handle cutting episodes well. Fear and shame consumed us. *Keep it a secret,* we determined. *Don't let anyone know.* What a difficult time.

In Reneé's junior year of high school, a counselor diagnosed her with clinical depression and several other mood disorders. A psychiatrist diagnosed her with a sensory processing disorder (SPD), also called sensory integration disorder (SID), an extreme sensitivity to external stimuli.

SPD, we learned, affected all of Reneé's senses, causing a feeling of angst and extreme irritation with things that didn't bother anyone else. A specialist who suffers with SPD herself says, "What is interesting, ho-hum, pleasurable, or exalting for most people can be irritating, disgusting, alarming, and even painful to [those suffering from SPD]."[4]

I was impatient and irritated with her much of the time. I felt overwhelmed with guilt when the SPD diagnosis was made. *You mean there's a physiological reason?* If only we had known. It would've made a huge difference. But we hadn't known.

If you don't yet know the cause for your child's behaviors, I encourage you to keep digging for a diagnosis. Be willing to humble yourself and ask for help. It may take more than one doctor or specialist to get to the root of the problem. And although finding a reason isn't necessarily the same as finding a solution, it will help you to grow in your understanding of the situation—and it also helps you to overcome the denial that isn't helping anyone.

The Stories We Tell Ourselves

How can parents come out of denial and begin to face these kinds of grueling challenges? There's one answer: we have no choice. The increasing seriousness of our children's problems forces us, kicking and screaming, into reality. No parents want to admit their child has serious issues. We don't want anything to be wrong. But denying the issues hurts everyone involved.

Reneé's sensitivities, cutting, smoking, depression, suicidal struggles, mental health issues, drinking, and drug abuse were uncovered bit by bit. As each one came to light, it was like peeling back the layers of an onion. These are a few of the clues we noticed. Look for them as warning signs in your child and be aware: you may be leaving denial behind any day now.

- expressions, verbal or written, of hopelessness and despair
- smelling peculiar, like marijuana, cigarette smoke, or alcohol
- lame excuses for arriving home late
- too much time spent alone in their room
- neglecting personal hygiene
- hanging out with questionable friends
- frequent lying
- listening to angry, depressing music
- increased use of crude language
- wearing all-black clothes often; drastic changes in makeup and hair color
- falling grades
- increased disrespect, anger, and rebellion
- loss of interest in activities previously enjoyed
- changes in usual sleep patterns

All of these gradually got our attention and convinced us something was amiss, but still we didn't grasp the depth of Reneé's issues for a while—not until she was seventeen. We took Reneé to a counselor, then a psychiatrist. (It's also good to see a family physician since there can be medical explanations for a child's behaviors.) The results of Reneé's evaluations peeled back the onion even more.

Yet my head stayed stuck in the sand like an ostrich's even when my daughter's worsening behaviors revealed her greater troubles: addictions to alcohol and drugs. *Sure, she's drinking some,* I told myself, *but it's not a problem. Using drugs? Maybe, but she's not an addict. She can't be.*

SURVIVING THE LOSS OF DENIAL

Harboring denial is like having an untreated wound. Ignoring it doesn't do any good. It only gets worse. Finally, traumatic, heartbreaking events yanked me out of denial and threw me into a new and foreign world of counselors, psychiatrists, medications, psych wards, behavioral hospitals, rehabs, and ER recovery rooms. *I can't believe it,* I kept telling myself. *I don't belong here.* But my eyes were finally opened the whole the way. *Pop!* Our idealistic bubble burst wide open.

One dad described a similar situation with his own family: "Naiveté or lack of awareness or just plain ignorance had been my cushion and suddenly there was nothing between me and the truth."[5]

When I cried out to God, He gave me the courage to stop denying and to start treating my wounds. He strengthened me to take one day at a time and enjoy one moment at a time while I kept doing what I knew to do: face the hard things, be honest with Him and with others, and run to Jesus. He provided what I needed—every time.

While I lived in the land of denial, I could go about my daily routine and pretend Reneé was okay. I could hang on to my fantasy that everything was fine; this was a phase she would grow out of. I mistakenly thought she was just different, unique. If I could simply hold on and persevere through the turbulent teen years, I believed things one day would be better. She'd snap out of it on her own.

Questions that had no answers plagued my mind during the day and night. What was going on with my daughter? Could there be an explanation? What was ahead? Could I handle it? But denial felt like a safe place to live. I would push back my concerns and doubts. *No, no. It's going to be all right.* However, choosing to leave denial behind was a two-edged sword—better and harder—for both of us.

Now I knew there was a problem, and it was much more than we ever imagined. The dreams we had for our daughter would have to change. The road to recovery would be long and hard. It would require a lot from us. We would have to see professionals and manage medications while watching her closely for additional signs of danger. Reality hurt badly. Yet it was comforting to know there was an explanation for her behaviors. We could do something about it—but not much. And no one could say how long it would take for positive change to occur.

Reneé still held all the cards—she would have to want help, to receive what was being offered, and to choose to cooperate. Learning to face what was really going on also made it possible for me to leave shame behind and really live again.

How many times have you cried out in despair, voicing a prayer like the one my doctor prayed over our newborn Reneé? When you call out to Him, He'll help. I promise. In the parable of the prodigal son (Luke 15:11–32), we see how eager God is to come to us in our time of need. He runs to meet us right where we are. What a beautiful picture.

How can you know if you're in denial?

- If others express concerns about things they see in your child that you don't and you keep saying, "It's okay. Nothing's wrong," you might be in denial. Playing that game is exhausting. But when you're too close to the situation, it can be difficult to get a clear view of what's really happening. We all have tunnel vision.
- If you have a nagging feeling that something's off, but you haven't had the courage to do anything about it, you might be in denial.

- If you find yourself holding back, not taking action because you're worried about your reputation, you might be in denial.
- If you're blaming yourself or making excuses for your child's behaviors, you might be in denial.

When I stopped denying Reneé had problems, it was easy to sink into a hole of self-condemnation, shame, and guilt. Climbing out was a slow, gradual process. *I'm a failure as a parent*, I thought. *If only I had done more of this and not that. Why didn't I see what was happening sooner?* Learning to be gentle with myself, talking honestly with others who understood, forgiving my mistakes, and accepting that I'd done the best I could came slowly. Toughening up and developing thicker skin helped me not to be bothered by what anyone else thought. God knew the truth and He understood. This was all that really mattered. In His eyes I wasn't a bad parent. He didn't blame me for anything. What a relief.

When you're ready for something healthier than denial, friend, cling to God. If you're not sure what you believe, now is a good time to make that a priority. Faith helps us endure and stay strong in life's storms. We need extra help from Someone bigger and greater than ourselves. Scripture says we're never alone: "God is our refuge and strength, an ever-present help in trouble. Therefore we will not fear. ... The Lord Almighty is with us" (Psalm 46:1–2, 7).

O God, give us wisdom and strength to be the best parents we can be. Help us be honest with ourselves, stop pretending, come out of our denial, face what is, and run to You. May Your will be done in our child's life— and in ours. Amen.

Scripture That Helps

My grace is sufficient for you, for my power is made perfect in weakness. (2 Corinthians 12:9)

As for me, I will always have hope. (Psalm 71:14)

5

Shock

"I'm sorry to have to make this call. But I have it on good report or I wouldn't call you. I haven't caught Mark, but I understand he's using marijuana."

I'll never forget the day. . . .

The news shattered me. The idea that my son, Mark, who was 16 and a junior in high school, could possibly have used drugs was the furthest thing from my mind. We had a good family. I never in my wildest imagination thought we would go down this road.

—Noy Sparks, *Hit by a Ton of Bricks*

Have you ever received an electrical shock when you plugged something in? I'm sure you recall what it felt like. How did you react? It always catches me by surprise and takes my breath away. What a perfect analogy for how I felt when I'd hear bad news about Reneé. I'd be going about my daily routine and suddenly—*zap*. It hurt a lot. Every time.

As a hurting parent, you've been on the receiving end of bad news about your son or daughter. You know exactly what I'm talking about. You understand the shock. You've experienced the way it sucks the air out of your lungs or makes your stomach drop. It's hard to forget.

Maybe you saw a few warning signs like the ones I mentioned in the previous chapter, but maybe not. If you did, then you probably tried everything in your power to save your child. Sometimes your efforts worked, other times they didn't. Each shock brought more heartache. Maybe for you the bad news has been relentless, like the constant pounding of waves on the seashore.

If only you could make it stop.

If only you knew how to help your child.

If only you could help yourself.

If only . . .

Recurring, distressing surprises can take their toll on our emotional health. Like unceasing waves, they began to erode my confidence as a mother. From the time Reneé was a toddler, her unpredictable moods and meltdowns kept me off balance. Sweet, loving, and cooperative one minute, Reneé could turn ornery, unruly, and defiant the next. I never knew what to expect. Some days I felt as if I was losing my mind. Other days were full of tantrums—hers and mine. Maybe you understand.

Many times you could find me on my knees next to my bed, pounding my fists on a pillow, salty tears of frustration streaming down my cheeks. How staggering to discover, over time, that our precious child was struggling with being bullied and having mental health issues and suicidal thoughts. And later, addiction and sexual trauma. Dazed, we could barely function. *This is just too much.*

THE DAMAGE OTHER KIDS CAN DO

The first shock came with the discovery that Reneé had been victimized by a bully from kindergarten through the second grade. We were alarmed and took immediate action as soon as we found out about it when she was in first grade. We were appalled to discover years later, when she was an adult, the harassment had continued for another year and a half and we never knew. *How could this happen?*[6]

THE CRIMSON RAIN: CUTTING

Self-injury was another shock. As I mentioned, Reneé started this habit at age twelve. We immediately wondered if she was trying to kill, not just harm, herself. We learned this was a myth: most self-injurers don't want to die. Melinda Smith and Jeanne Segal of HelpGuide.org addressed this myth in an online article and observed, "They are not trying to kill themselves—they are trying to cope with their pain. In fact, self-injury may be a way of helping themselves to go on living. However, in the long-term, people who self-injure have a much higher risk of suicide, which is why it's so important to seek help."[7]

MENTAL STORMS

In 2003 our family was living in Moscow as missionaries with Cru. About that time we noticed some worrisome behaviors with Reneé: with-drawing, wearing all black, making weak excuses for being late, smelling of cigarette smoke, writing about being despondent and wanting to die in a paper for school (although it was written in the third person, so it wasn't clear if she meant herself or not). She became an excellent actress, hiding her inner deep struggles. We had to know if our seventeen-year-old was a danger to herself. After a lot of prayer, on a cold fall day, we decided we'd sit down together with Reneé and over a cup of hot cocoa try to get some answers, no matter how long it took. This led to a long night of asking hard questions and waiting for honest answers. "Tell me what you're re-ally feeling about living here?" "Have you been feeling depressed? Hope-less?" "We know it's really hard to be honest, but please tell us, have you been hurting yourself?" "We read one of your poems for school and won-dered if you were expressing your true feelings in it? Maybe it reveals something you need to tell us?" "Have you been thinking about taking your life?" "Tell me more about that."

By the end of the night, Reneé reluctantly confided, "Mom, Dad, I didn't want to hurt you. I never wanted you to know, but I've been feeling so down I started to hurt myself—and, yes, I wanted to take my life."

Zap. Oh, how this stings! I never suspected my daughter felt this bad. We expressed empathy and sadness over her despair. We affirmed her

Reneé: On Bullying

Look for warning signs, such as significant changes in your child's behavior. As with kids developing a substance addiction, they may . . .

- become aggressive and hateful toward their friends
- say mean things to you or to siblings
- withdraw and isolate
- try to hide unexplained bruises
- have a short fuse, anger easily, or be hypersensitive
- appear depressed or lethargic
- comment that they wish they could go to sleep and never wake up
- make up excuses to not go to school
- experience sleep disturbances, nightmares, or insomnia
- change the way they dress

After the bullying started, I changed my behavior. I began dressing more like a tomboy. Maybe I did this to make myself appear stronger or tougher so that the bullying would stop. Bullies mocked just about every part of my body. I was thin and kids called me names like Spider Legs, so I stopped wearing shorts until I was seventeen. I started wearing glasses in the fifth grade and it didn't bother me at all—until someone made fun of me in the sixth grade. I didn't wear glasses again until I was twenty-five. These are just a few examples, but bullying affected me in many ways long after the behavior had stopped.

for how well she'd adjusted to a foreign culture and the great attitude she'd had for the previous eighteen months.

After that night we made the decision to move back to the States as fast as we could. *That's all she needs,* we reasoned, *and a few sessions with a counselor.* We were so naive.

Pay attention to what your kids are drawing or reading, what music they listen to, what television shows they watch, and what social media they participate in—look for violent or troubling themes. They may subconsciously seek to desensitize themselves to what they've experienced to make it seem like it's not such a big deal.

Show your kids their voices matter, that they can affect things when they speak. Show them you are listening, and let them know that you will take action to protect them as best you can. Tell your child you believe them and you want to hear about what's happening, that you will do everything in your power to protect and help them. Don't just get angry about the situation and tell them you're sorry. Do something. Go to the school (or to wherever the harassment is taking place) and inform the responsible adults; recruit help to bring it to an end. This is essential for your child's well-being. If at all possible, calmly talk to the bully's parents or guardian to inform them about what's going on and get their help to make it stop. Research this topic to equip your child to deal with the situation and find out what your options are. Some parents have withdrawn their children from public school and chosen homeschooling or virtual school until their child was older and more capable of defending themselves. They took this step only after repeated unsuccessful attempts to obtain assistance from school personnel and because of how their child was being adversely affected.[8] If your child knows you'll do these things when they're having troubles, they will be more likely to talk to you about them.

Within a few weeks we were sitting in a counselor's office. She gently told us, "Your daughter needs a psychiatric evaluation." *What?* Not long after that is when we received the diagnosis that Reneé was suffering from bipolar disorder or SPD, as mentioned in the previous chapter. *Zap. Zap.*

The psychiatrist's next words have haunted my memory ever since: "My main concern is that Reneé is seriously depressed. On a scale of one to ten, ten being normal or feeling fine, and one being suicidal, she's a

Reneé: On Self-Injury

Be aware of the warning signs. Along with the usual distress signs in teens, such as isolation and long periods of time spent alone in their rooms, look for the following:

- A lack of self-love or low self-esteem. Some signs or indicators to look for would be negative, judgmental, or dismissive language when they talk about themselves, their struggles, or their feelings; comparing themselves to their peers or to unrealistic standards; and constantly putting the needs of others before their own to the extent that they never offer anything to themselves. They may not make healthy choices for themselves but are okay with what anyone else wants or needs from them. They spend time or make friends with people who don't treat them well or respect them.
- Depression.
- Isolation from friends and family.
- Spending a lot of time alone in the bathroom.
- A sudden shortage of bandages.

one or a two. It's a miracle she's still alive." Actual waves of shock swept over me.

I felt as though a bomb had gone off under my chair. I held Tom's hand tighter, squeezing until it turned blue. Everything around me shifted into slow motion. *I think I'm going to scream and cry and run out of the room all at the same time. Mental illness? Suicidal? Please, God, let this be a bad dream. Wake me up—now.*

The shock has lessened over the years, yet some moments you never

- Your child wearing long sleeves in warm weather.
- Sensitivity to touch (they may cut in various places).

If you find out your child is cutting, talk about it in a nonthreatening way. Create a safe environment by listening without getting angry. Kids need to express how they're feeling without a parent overreacting or underreacting by saying "That's not so bad," "You weren't really cutting yourself—that's not what happened," or trying to fix, solve, or correct them. Don't punish them for their pain. It's significant. Don't be invalidating or dismissive. They won't talk to you again. Offer options for talking to someone else, such as a therapist or another trusted adult.

Information plus application equals transformation. By educating yourself and refusing to minimize the situation, you open up a line of communication with your child. By checking in with your child and asking questions, you will transform how both of you experience the situation. Ultimately, it allows you to love yourself, because you're doing the most loving thing you can. And you're giving your child permission to do the same—to show up, to choose (to answer you honestly or not), and by applying these things, to change what's going on.

Mom, Dad, your kids are worth it. They matter. There is help. There is hope. Never give up, and don't let them give up on themselves.

entirely forget. A friend of mine described her experience when she and her husband first learned of their daughter's mental health diagnosis:

> We were stunned, yet relieved, because it explained some of the bizarre behavior our child exhibited. Although we were always advocates for emancipating and launching our children, we were not aware that mental illness was such a common occurrence. Like most, we were under the delusion that our parenting skills would be able to make near-perfect children and that we had control over the outcomes.

I'm not going to talk in too much detail about Reneé's mental health issues. They're part of her private story to tell if she chooses to do so one day, but she has some great insights.

OUR BEST IS IMPERFECT

Tom and I fully admit we aren't perfect parents. That's impossible. There's only one perfect parent—God—and look at all the trouble His children have caused Him, especially His first two: Adam and Eve. In Genesis 2–3 we learn they lived in a perfect world, they had no sin nature (they hadn't bitten into the forbidden fruit yet), no peer pressure, no modern temptations, no problems—nothing amiss. And yet they still chose to rebel. It was the inevitable outcome of being given a free will by their Maker.

Did God do anything wrong? No.

Did He make any mistakes in His parenting? Emphatically no.

If He, being all-powerful and all-wise, couldn't make even His first two children behave, then why do we expect any better from ourselves? Who are we to deserve better than God? *Wow. That puts it in a whole different perspective, doesn't it?* And while I realize that now, I didn't see it that way when problems with Reneé first started showing up.

In those early days, when each new issue Reneé faced became known, shock paralyzed me emotionally. Who could understand? Who could I talk to? How could I cope? I withdrew in guilt and fear and soon found isolation only made the journey harder. As I met more parents going through similar things, they kept telling me that it was to my advantage to not suffer alone. They told me how much it had helped them when they began to reach out and stopped isolating themselves. They urged me to do the hard thing and find a support group. Getting involved in these helped me resist the urge to isolate even more. They encouraged us to keep talking and connecting with others who understood.

I'm so glad I listened. I longed for an extreme makeover for my daughter, but you know what? I needed one as much as she did. Through becoming informed, talking to safe people (people who accepted me in my mess without judging, were confidential and trustworthy, who didn't

Reneé: On Mental Illness

I erroneously believed it wouldn't do any good if my parents knew the truth about my struggles, so I convinced myself that my feelings were normal. I was overwhelmed with anxiety and self-hatred. My mind would be a storm of sharp negativity, things I never realized about myself at the time. I have no idea where they came from. I felt like I was a bad person, helplessly alone and unlovable, even on a good day in the company of friends. I felt the heavy weight of depression, and it was exhausting. I felt isolated and broken and I didn't understand why. I'd experience extreme bursts of anger, sadness, and a crazed kind of energy and happiness that seemed beyond my control, beyond reason.

(continued on the next page)

I'd often walk home from school, beating myself up for acting hyper, talking too much, and doing things I later thought were stupid or embarrassing. I would vow to be more quiet, controlled, and serious going forward. Sometimes I had a disturbing apathy toward life, contemplating suicide in the sixth grade. I remember bringing sleeping pills to school so I could take them and sleep all day, then I wouldn't have to deal with the pain I felt.

The hard part was feeling so many things so strongly but not having any real understanding as to why. If asked why I felt like I did, a reasonable answer would have been, "I feel really depressed." But I didn't always have an answer, or the answer didn't seem sufficient enough for how extreme the feeling was. At other times I feared expressing my feelings when they weren't true of how I felt all the time. I would feel that way intensely, but then in a few days, or even in a few hours, I would feel something else entirely.

I didn't want to be held to one feeling or treated differently because of it when I might move out of it soon. I think I also feared being punished for my feelings. I'm not sure where that came from. It's still something I work on today, but now I know that the kind of crazy, unfathomable love God has for us is never one that punishes us for our feelings. And that has helped me so much.

For a long time I thought everyone felt the same way I did, at least sometimes. I didn't think it was that bad, either. But I believed I had to hide my struggles and pretend I was okay to protect my parents. I couldn't let them know the truth. I couldn't disappoint them.

I had no idea there was anyone who could help me.

When I started wearing black all the time, I wanted my outer appearance to match how I felt inside. The dark color represented my inner turmoil, sadness, depression, and hopelessness.

If your child has been diagnosed with a mental illness, don't panic.

It's not a death sentence. A diagnosis simply means there's a name for what your child is going through; it will provide a better understanding of the issues your child is facing and how to help. Remember that this diagnosis or illness is not who your child is—don't let it define him or her. You can do this by helping your child understand their diagnosis is more like a lens to look through. It's kind of like footnotes that help explain what you just read or a manual that tells you how this car or this machine specifically works.

It's not a summation of who they are or what their life is all about, but a means for the people who love them—the people who want to help them—to better understand how they work. It helps identify some of their parts and says "Ah, so this part of you seems to work this way" or "Oh, this is your language" so you can communicate better. To me, a diagnosis simply means there's a name or word for what I'm experiencing, I'm not the only one experiencing it, and I have a way to talk about it. It means I and others might be able to know what I need to work best, how they can help me and love me well.

A simple way of not letting a mental health diagnosis be this big, scary thing is by talking about it—not making it a hush-hush taboo subject—asking and inviting questions and keeping it in the light. When we learn and grow together, fear won't have any room to instill guilt, shame, or lies.

I encourage you and your child to educate yourselves about the diagnosis and keep an open line of communication so you can walk through this side by side.

Allow the diagnosis to be an affirmation. You have received this information because you can handle it, because it will help you and your child. Remind your child that they are not alone, that getting help (therapy, medication, and so on) is not a sign of weakness in character or faith but rather of strength.

lecture or look down on or make me feel guilty), journaling about my feelings, and praying a lot, I found the courage to seek help from professionals and others. In time I came to better understand Reneé's behavior and made peace with the uncomfortable situation—I accepted the truth that I couldn't fix my daughter or make any of the bad things go away.

Reneé was an addict. She would always have to manage her temptations. She suffered with mental health issues. There was no cure, but she could learn to cope and have a wonderful, good life in spite of it. So could I.

By letting go of what I couldn't change, I began to change.

I became more tolerant and compassionate and less judgmental toward others who struggled with these issues. Before this happened to our family, I realized I felt above it, better than *them*. I looked down on *those* parents, making unfair assumptions, the kind I resent today. I became much more humble, laying down spiritual pride. I wasn't the perfect Christian parent after all. I didn't have the answers. I grew stronger exponentially in my relationship with the Lord and my understanding of the Scriptures. Little problems didn't bother me so much anymore. My relationships grew stronger and deeper with my husband, our other children, and my friends. I appreciated the small joys of life in fresh, new ways.

A + B = ?

Another helpful biblical insight is found in Isaiah 5:1–7 in the story of a man (representing God) who planted a vineyard. He did everything right according to the *Farmer's Almanac:* cleared out all the stones, planted in fertile ground at the best time of year, used the healthiest seeds, pulled the weeds, and watered regularly. Then he built a watchtower for protection and prepared to enjoy the rewards of his hard work.

When harvest time came, "he looked for a crop of good grapes, but it yielded only bad fruit" (verse 2). Verse 4 records his discouragement:

"What more could have been done for my vineyard than I have done for it? When I looked for good grapes, why did it yield only bad?" He pleads, "Can you think of anything I could have done to my vineyard that I didn't do?" (verse 4, MSG). The farmer did everything required for an excellent crop, yet look what he got.

The Bible affirms doing everything by the book doesn't always produce the desired results. Neither Tom nor I understood this in the beginning. We thought if we tried hard enough to be perfect parents, we'd get perfect children. Guess what? It doesn't work that way.

If anything, it puts more pressure on our offspring to be what they can never be—faultless. They end up feeling inadequate, as if they can't be good enough to deserve our acceptance.

In parenting, there's no mathematical equation to ensure a certain outcome. In addition, one plus one always equals two. But in child rearing, there are no absolutes. Sometimes one plus one equals two, but at other times it might equal three or sixty-three. A plus B doesn't always equal C. You might get Z. It's true. If anyone tells you, "Follow these instructions: do this and this and you'll get the child you always wanted," don't believe it. That person is misinformed. Remember God's experience as a parent.

Processing the shock of what I've been through has been demanding. At a loss to know how to respond to innumerable traumatic surprises, I found depression coming over me like a dark shadow. Trying to dig out of the darkness, I discovered a few things that can help all of us.

Choose to Remember the Good Times

You did have some. Try not to dwell only on the negative.

Remember, God Makes No Mistakes

He chose you to be your son or daughter's parent. You can rely on Him to equip you for the job.

Accept That You Didn't Do It All Right

Stop trying to be a superhuman, model parent. Don't be ashamed. Do you know anyone who's perfect at anything? Such a person doesn't exist. We need to own any part we may have played in our children's problems—our failures, mistakes, and clumsiness—ask forgiveness from God and from them, where appropriate, for being too harsh, for not being consistent enough to follow through with rules and consequences, for being too weak to give discipline when it was needed for fear of losing the relationship, for trying to be their friend instead of their parent, for not being able to understand them or their struggles, for not trying hard enough because you were too angry and hurt, for overreacting out of fear when you saw worrisome behaviors and had a strong need to protect them from potential danger, for pushing them too hard to be perfect or be what you wanted them to be. Maybe going to college was your dream, not theirs, and you forced it on them. Maybe you pushed them into a certain activity with a lot of pressure to perform and succeed, and they didn't really like it but never felt they could tell you. Don't get stuck there. Forgive yourself too. That may be hardest of all.

Be Reasonable

Relax your expectations of your child, yourself, and everyone else in your life. Trust God with the outcome as you pray and figure out what's reasonable. It's not easy. A professional can provide insights. You did your best. It may be time to leave the results in the hands of the professionals and the One who can help you with anything—He really is in control, even when it doesn't look like it.

Go Easy on Yourself

God gave no parenting rule book to follow, but He encourages us to ask for the help we need: "If any of you lacks wisdom, you should ask God, who gives generously to all without finding fault, and it will be given to you" (James 1:5). He'll give courage and strength to process your feelings: "The LORD gives strength to his people; the LORD blesses his people with peace" (Psalm 29:11). As you grow in peace, you can move toward acceptance.

It's not easy, but you can do it. We're so brutally hard on ourselves. Remind yourself often that no one is perfect. You did your best in a difficult situation. You were unprepared to face the issues you encountered. You could never have anticipated them. You probably couldn't have done any better than you did, without any experience or forewarning. Give yourself the grace you probably offer others. The only one who expects perfection of you is you. Besides, if God can forgive us, can't we do the same?

IMPERFECTIONS AND ALL

As time went by, we faced many more shocking situations. Each hit hard, leaving us bewildered and shaken. Many times I wondered if I would survive. Have you wondered the same thing? If you have, you might like to use the following prayer:

> *God, I don't know how to do this. I feel as though You made a big mistake when You chose me to be _____'s parent. I'm not wise enough or strong enough for the job. I can't do it without You, but I believe You're big enough and strong enough to help us both. Show me how to process the shocking things I've experienced. I don't want to keep secrets anymore. Thank You for caring about me and my child. Amen.*

Today, Tom, Reneé, and I are able to love and accept each other as we are, imperfections and all. We've been humble and honest about our shortcomings and our need to rely on God. We're grateful for this openness we share. How liberating it's been. It's okay to not be okay. We can be real. We can be human. So can you!

Scripture That Helps

Trust in the LORD with all your heart and do not lean on your own understanding. In all your ways acknowledge Him, and He will make your paths straight. (Proverbs 3:5–6, NASB)

For great is his love toward us, and the faithfulness of the LORD endures forever. Praise the LORD. (Psalm 117:2)

6

Fear and Worry

When we are powerless to do a thing, it is a great joy that we can come and step inside the ability of Jesus.

—Corrie ten Boom

When we come out of denial about our child's struggles and learn to process shock, we may feel the way this parent did: "I can't think. All is muddled. I want to sink into sleep, to escape. I am so tired. To care about anything takes such a tremendous effort. The fog keeps rolling in."⁹

I felt that way, and so did Reneé.

Tom and I were on a mission to save our daughter's life—but how? We had no idea. We trusted God to show us the way. She was fighting a battle and so were we. Fear became my closest friend and my worst enemy. And worry came hand in hand with the fear. Their slimy tentacles pulled me into a deep pit.

When we decided to return to America from Russia, we let Reneé decide where we would live. April deeply loved her sister and understood enough of what was going on that she was in full agreement of whatever Reneé would choose. Michael had graduated from college and was living on his own, so he wasn't affected by the decision. Reneé chose Orlando since it was our last stateside home. Guided by a trusted friend, we quickly found a counselor who sounded like a good fit. We began to relax, convinced this would fix everything.

What a mistake for us to think this way. The counselor was a great fit, but we soon learned that the problem of self-injury is so deep, especially once it becomes an addiction, that it takes much more than meeting with a therapist for a few months for the destructive behavior to stop.

Knowing your beloved child is cutting herself is horrible. I couldn't stand to see her wounds. Each one pierced my own heart. If you've dealt with this, you know how terrifying it can be. You live in a constant state of fright, always on high alert, watching for warning signs, anxiety overflowing around the clock. Worry is formidable. There's no rest from the torment.

Compelled to keep Reneé safe, we hid every sharp object. At least we tried to hide them all. If your child is a cutter, you know. Our children go to great lengths to hide the evidence, and they are brilliant at it. Some indicators to look for are bloody Kleenex in the trash in their bedroom or bathroom; bloodstains on their sheets, pillowcases, or clothes; spending longer amounts of time than usual in their bedroom or bathroom; scratch marks on their arms or legs for which they have unlikely explanations; or they're wearing long sleeves when it's not cool (I've mentioned this before). But remember, the whole point is that self-injury is a highly private, secret matter. You shouldn't expect to notice these things unless they want you to. If that happens, then Reneé says this is their way of letting you know they *want* you to ask about it. It's a nonverbal cry for help. So if your child allows you to see any marks on their arms or somewhere else, *do* ask about it. "I noticed those marks on your arm. Are you okay? What happened? Did you hurt yourself? I'm sorry you're feeling so bad inside. Would you like to talk about it? I'd love to listen. If you'd rather not talk to me, then maybe you could talk with a counselor? You know it's okay to need to talk to someone about things you're struggling with. Sometimes we all need a little extra help."

Reneé's struggles were compounded when she began drinking and abusing her medications. Of course, we were clueless. Most parents are.

We even wrestled with the idea of taking her bedroom door off the hinges. It worked for other families we knew. Maybe it could help us.

"Oh, Tom, I'm so afraid Reneé might hurt herself seriously. I could never forgive myself. Should we take her bedroom door off?"

"I don't know, honey. Maybe it's worth trying, but then it might just make things worse. She could end up hating us more than she already does. That thought is unbearable too. I hate being the bad guys all the time."

"Me, too, and there's no guarantee it will work. If she's determined to cut, she'll still find a way. With her other mental health factors, it feels more complicated and dangerous. What if it makes her so upset that she ends up doing something worse? Maybe it's not worth the risk."

In the end, we couldn't do it.

LIVING WITH SOMEONE DRAWN TOWARD DEATH

Every time Reneé went in the bathroom, I'd start counting the minutes, listening for her to come out, tortured by the idea of what she might be doing. If your child has an eating disorder, drug problem, or suicidal tendencies, you've experienced the same thing. *I have to stop her. What if she goes too far this time? What if she does permanent damage or even kills herself?*

When it felt as if she'd been in there too long, I'd knock on the door. "Reneé, are you done yet? You need to help me with the dishes," I'd say as calmly as possible. Any excuse would do. We got pretty good at making them up. Knowing her problems were complicated by suicidal thoughts, Tom and I were a mess.

If you're like me, you start the day wondering, *How is she feeling today? What kind of mood is she in? What clothes is she wearing? How dark is her makeup? Does she look upset? Should I ask her about it? No, it might make her want to hurt herself more. Is she thinking about taking her life? Should I bring it up? I couldn't live with myself if I caused her to . . . Don't say a word. It's safer that way.*

You begin to scrutinize everything your child does and everyone they spend time with. Of course, your child seems to detest your efforts and wants complete freedom, no questions or explanations. They fight you every step of the way, lying and sneaking off to do whatever they want. It's exhausting.

The typical parental inquiries—"Where are you going tonight?" "What are your plans?" "Who's going?" "I don't know if that's such a good idea." "I don't know anything about that person"—draw the inevitable responses—"Come on, Mom." "Give me a break." "I feel like I'm in prison." "Whatever." You become the enemy, but that's the way it has to be. At least for now.

Our goal is to help our children get well and hope they don't make mistakes with long-term, negative consequences. Every decision feels critical. Tom and I had many tense conversations late into the night over these issues. We wrestled endlessly over what to do, working hard to agree on every decision. Like you, we desperately wanted to do the right thing. But what was it? That's exactly the problem; no one really knows. Our counselor would say, "You're the adults. You figure it out." We hated that. We desperately needed someone to tell us what to do because we had no idea. We looked for parenting books we liked and did our best to follow their guidance.[10] We also went to a conference for hurting parents and gleaned a lot of wisdom from others who were ahead of us on the journey. But it was still really difficult. Every decision was intense. How we wished God would've handed out a guidebook to parents with detailed instructions for every situation we might encounter. Wouldn't that be great? But there is no such book. Rats.

DREADING THE MORNING

"Reneé, honey, one wrong choice could have catastrophic consequences, altering your future," we told her. "We don't want that to happen. We only want to help you move in the right direction so you can fulfill your dreams." *Can't you see we're not against you? We're trying to help.*

When Reneé wasn't doing well, I dreaded opening her door in the morning, wondering if she'd become despondent in the night. After all, a psychiatrist had told us, "Untreated depression is the number one cause of suicide." She hadn't been on the medication long enough for it to have had any beneficial effect yet. What if? Would I find her lying in a pool of her own blood? Would she be dead or alive? Finally I said, "I can't do this anymore, Tom. It's killing me. We've got to take turns going into her room in the morning."

And so we did. Afflicted by nightmares, I found any sleep I managed to get far from peaceful. Every day we faced the unthinkable possibility. Maybe you have too. We wondered, *How do we live like this? Will we ever feel normal again? What is normal?* I wasn't so sure I knew anymore. *Oh, God, please save our daughter.*

Psychiatric terms and the lingo of addiction and rehab were foreign to us because they had never been part of our life experience before. Now we needed to learn this new language, because with no comprehension of their meaning, we found the terms created more fear and anxiety. How awkward, strange, and uncomfortable to hear those terms used in reference to our daughter: alcoholism, detox, self-mutilation, brain disorders, dual-diagnosis, suicidal.

Is this really our life?

The psychiatrist's words, "It's a miracle she's still alive," altered my world. The day we sat in his office to hear the diagnosis, he gave us several medications for Reneé to try, along with directions and phone numbers if we had any questions or problems. The pill bottles were given to us in a small brown paper bag, the same kind she took her lunch in to school. Only now, instead of a sandwich, fruit, and a cookie, it held Seroquel and Paxil. The irony felt cruel.

It rained when we left the doctor's office that day, shortly after returning from Russia. *The sky's crying. That's what I want to do. And never stop.* My thoughts swirled with questions that would remain for the next decade. *What's going to happen next? How long will it take for her to feel better? What do we do if these medications don't work? How do we keep her safe? How do we sleep at night and survive this?*

Have you walked in my shoes?

At first, your child may have cooperated with taking the multicolored pills, as Reneé did. Once she realized her emotional state wasn't normal, she genuinely appeared to want to feel better. But many drugs prescribed for mental health issues bring unpleasant, unavoidable side effects. The day came when Reneé stopped the meds. (Are you nodding your head?) This is a common problem for those living with mental illness—not co-operating with their treatment plans. This escalates a parent's sense of impending doom. Uncontrollable worry sweeps over you, along with guilt, sorrow, and shame. Together they engulf your heart. But when we educate and inform ourselves, develop a support network, process our feelings, and take care of ourselves, we begin to control these feelings. They become more manageable. They no longer overcome us. Once we better understand self-injury, addiction, and our child's mental health issue or brain disorder, we'll see there's no need to be ashamed. We realize our child's problems have nothing to do with us, unless we've intentionally contributed to them in some way. We can let go of guilt, knowing it's not our fault.

We still have concerns, but worry doesn't consume us. We find new strength and comfort from the community we surround ourselves with. We still feel sad, but it's not as consuming. Of course this doesn't happen all at once, but you can begin to cope when you start doing these things. Take a minute and look at Corrie ten Boom's quote at the beginning of this chapter. When we feel like we can't do something—like any of the suggestions I've given—we can find the ability to do it from Jesus. That's where I found it.

CLOSE CALL

After about six months back in the States, Reneé's solution was to self-medicate with more alcohol and drugs—unbeknown to us—to numb her relentless inner pain. At eighteen she moved out, lived on the streets, took a nosedive into addiction, ended up in psych wards and behavioral hospitals for severe cutting and suicide attempts, spent time in numerous rehabs, and experienced gut-wrenching relapses. Countless times her life hung in the balance. Sometimes we knew, other times we didn't, but we knew about enough of them to last a lifetime. Since she was eighteen, we no longer had any control or authority over her. She was free to do as she chose. We couldn't stop her, as much as we wanted to.

Five years later, when Reneé was twenty-three, she came back home for a short period. The time finally came when we received another alarming middle-of-the-night phone call. We were out of town and she had been struggling; it's unreal how often these crises occurred when we were away. At 2:30 a.m., Tom's cell phone rang. His caller ID showed the name of Reneé's current counselor, which made our hearts race faster. *Oh, no, what's happened now?*

"Hello, Ray, what's wrong?" Tom said, full of trepidation.

"Mr. Yohe, I'm so sorry to bother you at this hour, but Reneé's in a crisis. I'm concerned for her safety. I had to call 911 and ask them to send the police to your home. Tom, I don't mean to overly alarm you, but when they went to your house, they couldn't get anyone to come to the door. They told me they rang the bell over and over. They knocked as hard as they could, but they still couldn't get anyone to answer. They even went around the side of the house and tried to look in the bedroom windows. They pounded on them too, but nothing."

Oh, God, no.

Panic-stricken, Tom said, "Oh, my gosh. Dena's dad and our dog are there too. One of them should've heard something. The dog usually barks her head off when anyone comes to the door. I can't imagine what's happened."

"Tom, you and Dena need to get home as fast as you can. I'll tell the police you're on your way. How long will it take you?"

"We're on the east coast, so it'll take at least an hour and a half. There's no one who can go for us, since Michael's three hours away in West Palm and April lives in Daytona. We really don't want to burden anyone else."

"I'm not at liberty to share any specifics due to patient-counselor confidentiality, but I can tell you this: imagine your daughter sitting in the middle of a room, drenched with kerosene, and she's holding a lit match. Mr. Yohe, I'm afraid she's on the verge of dropping it."

"We'll get there as soon as we can, and I'll call you when we pull into the driveway."

On the brink of hysteria, we launched into overdrive, tossed our belongings into our suitcases, and sprinted for the car. I called my dear friend and mentor, Suzanne. I knew she'd understand. I had called her in the wee hours of the night on many occasions over the years. She encouraged us and prayed with us on speakerphone almost the whole way home. God used her to help us keep our sanity that night. I couldn't believe Tom didn't get a speeding ticket. We practiced what we would say to explain our situation to a highway patrolman if we were stopped: "It's a life-and-death emergency. It's the truth, officer."

When we pulled into the driveway, our home looked empty. All was quiet. No police car was in sight. The officers had given up after a second attempt to rouse anyone. From the outside, everything looked peaceful. Tom mustered up the courage to open the front door and hurried to the back corner of the house where Reneé's room was situated. Hanging back, terrified at what we might find, I whispered, "Honey, I can't," and stayed in the living room.

After a few minutes he called out, "Dena, I think she's okay. Come quick."

Rushing to the doorway of her room, I still felt afraid to enter. Reneé was sprawled facedown on the bed's crumpled covers, fully dressed, her dyed-black hair disheveled. She appeared to be sleeping. But was she? Tom bent over again to check. We had to be sure. Cautiously, he felt her neck for a pulse while I held my breath.

Thank God, she was alive. I almost collapsed from the release of emotion. Anger and frustration immediately came to the forefront as we tried to wake her up—this has been a difficult task since she was a preteen. After Tom tried with no results, it was my turn. Reeking from the putrid smell of liquor and stale cigarette smoke, she finally rallied enough to assure us she was all right. We checked her pupils like Ray had instructed, hoping we did it right. *I'm so glad you're alive, Reneé, but I'm so stinking mad at you. You have no idea what we went through tonight.*

She moved out again soon after this incident. We couldn't live like that. She understood.

We were so angry with Reneé that night. Anger can become a big problem for parents like us, turning into uncontrolled outbursts. How have you coped with your anger? Maybe you have no problem expressing yours, calmly saying how you feel. But maybe you scream and yell, throw things, or even become physical. If you have difficulty in this area, your anger can turn into rage with the potential for violence. You may have said or done things you regretted later. But the damage has been done. You can't take it back. One mom told me, "I know it's wrong, but my son makes me so furious, I lose control and hit him. I feel terrible, but I don't know what else to do when I feel so mad. He knows all my hot buttons and seems to enjoy pushing me beyond my limits whenever he has the opportunity. I feel like I'm going crazy!"

Some of us have trouble appropriately expressing our angry feelings. We rant and rave at our child, but it doesn't do any good. Neither do endless lectures or arguments. While others aren't comfortable in expressing their anger, we're afraid of it. So we stuff it. We have our fits and tantrums internally, in our heads and in our dreams. We need to find a better way too, or our anger will turn into depression.

Anger isn't bad or wrong, but it can lead to bigger problems if not handled properly. We already have enough of those, don't we?

Here are a few ways you can try to cope with anger:

- If you like to write, record your feelings in a journal or write your child a letter saying everything you want to say. Then destroy it. Tear the letter to shreds. Stomp on it. Cut it up. Burn it. Do what feels satisfying.

- If you like to draw, create a picture expressing your rage. Don't judge or overanalyze yourself. Just do it.

- Give yourself permission to have a temper tantrum. Plan a time and place when you're all alone—so you won't frighten anyone—and let it go. Scream and yell, rant and rave, pound your fists, stomp your feet, cuss. Do whatever feels good. Just let your angry feelings out.

- Get physical: take a walk, go for a run, swim in a pool, take up kickboxing, lift weights, take a spin class, ride a bike, go to the gym, hit a punching bag.

- Talk with your safe people. Tell them what you're feeling. Hold nothing back. Vent and blow off some steam. You'll be glad you did.

These are positive ways to release pent-up anger and negative emotions, different types of emotional release valves. I encourage you to try a few of them and see which ones help.

As it turned out that almost fateful night, Reneé's grandfather was sleeping so soundly he never knew anything happened. We discovered that at age eighty-nine, his hearing was worse than we thought. We decided it would be too distressing for him to know, so we never told him. And our dog, well, it turned out her hearing wasn't so good, either.

One of the things I look back on from this event and give thanks for was having such an understanding friend I could call. The whole experience would have been much more difficult without her. This is a perfect example of the value of having a strong, caring community around you. It's worth all the effort it takes to develop. Their strength and support make all the difference in times of crisis. If you haven't already done so, I hope you'll begin to build this into your life.

FRETTING OVER THE PAST AND THE FUTURE

If only I could go back in time and do things differently.

If only I had been smarter.

If only I could have understood my child's struggles.

If only I had recognized the warning signs of her troubles.

If only I had checked in with her more thoroughly: "You look down today, can we talk about that?" "Tell me what wearing black means to you." "Please help me understand what's going on inside your heart."

Parents, if you're like me, maybe you don't really want to know.

Reneé: How Is Your Heart?

It would have been helpful if my parents had asked me what I was feeling more often and without taking it personally, trying to fix me, or judging my feelings. Just asking about my heart. I think the question "How is your heart?" allows us to talk about how we feel without the pressure to say why or disclose details unless we want to. I've learned to ask this of others, and I see I respond much better to it than "How are you?" or "Do you want to talk?" or "How are you doing with that?" Asking "What's so bad? Why?" and so on or comparing external circumstances to mine only felt like I was being told my feelings weren't justified, that they weren't valid or reasonable (which I already felt).

You're afraid to hear the truth. I was. Don't beat yourself up. It doesn't do any good to carry that weight of guilt over past mistakes. It only creates more misery for us and everyone around us. As I said earlier, we need to forgive ourselves and let go of our fears.

But how?

Stop Worry at the Physical Level

Stop and look in a mirror. Notice the tension in your forehead and eyes, your clenched jaw, frown, and stooped posture. We carry worry's tension in our bodies. Take three deep breaths—deep and slow—in through the nose and out through the mouth. This slows the pulse, clears the mind, and relaxes tight muscles. When we worry, we tend to hold our breath. Shallow, short breaths can heighten anxiety, and that's the last thing we need. So take in more oxygen. It enhances an overall feeling of well-being.

Get Moving

Take a long walk. Connecting with the beauty and wonder of nature is calming. Really look at the sky. It's a beautiful reminder of how great and powerful God is. Soak in a warm bath. Vigorous exercise and massages can also release worry. We need to find what we like and make ourselves do it. The psalmist said, "When my anxious thoughts multiply within me, your consolations delight my soul" (Psalm 94:19, NASB). Take some time to find what consoles you most when you're worried.

Get Gratitude or Become Grateful

I know it sounds odd when you're in the midst of life-altering circumstances, but I'll say it anyway: cultivate a grateful heart. Thankfulness is a good antidote for worry since it's difficult to be anxious and grateful at the same time. It puts worry in the proper perspective. You could also look for someone who needs help, and see how you can come to his or her

aid. This will boost your spirit, distract you from your troubles, and remind you of your many blessings.

Ask for More Faith

Trust God and ask for increased faith to trust Him more—He's worthy
of your trust—as well as the supportive people around you. Bad things do
happen, but we can be confident that whatever happens we'll be given
what we need to handle the situation. Boost your trust muscles by reading the Gospels and the book of Acts to remind yourself about the miracles of Jesus and the power of God. The Old Testament is also full of
amazing stories of what He can do.

Lay Down Your Burden

Turn it over to God in prayer: "Cast your burden upon the LORD and He
will sustain you" (Psalm 55:22, NASB). Focusing on Him and meditating
on His Word can soothe our minds and ease our souls. Read a psalm
every day, when you wake up and again before bed. His words are good
medicine for a fearful heart: "Even when walking through the dark valley of death I will not be afraid, for you are close beside me, guarding,
guiding all the way" (Psalm 23:4, TLB). Write favorite verses on index
cards and look at them often. By doing this, you'll remember two important things: how great God is and that you can put down whatever you're
carrying.

Turn Your Worries into Prayers

Take fearful thoughts and form them into conversations with God. We
need to give our worries to Him as soon as we realize they're building up.
Release those thoughts by handing them over to the only One who can
do anything about them. He'll hold them for us. "Don't worry about
anything; instead, pray about everything. Tell God what you need, and
thank him for all he has done. Then you will experience God's peace,

which exceeds anything we can understand. His peace will guard your hearts and minds as you live in Christ Jesus" (Philippians 4:6–7, NLT).

Find Safe Relationships

I said it earlier, but it's worth repeating: instead of isolating, reach out to others. Get community. When we're ready to talk, we need to confide in a few understanding friends. You may be surprised how many people are going through the same thing you are, but they're too embarrassed to tell anyone. Why do we persist in thinking we're the only ones?

Who's safe? Those people who won't think less of us when we spill our guts without censorship; they won't offer trite platitudes or attempt to explain our situation in a way that feels like preaching or lecturing. Safe people are good, empathetic listeners who will accept us and our children with all our messiness. They've probably had their own messes to deal with. Their bubble's been burst too. People who've suffered in some way will be the best equipped to help (support groups are a great place to find them). They tend to be more compassionate and understanding. Their faith has been tested by the trials of life and they've come through stronger. They've grown comfortable with their humanity. They're willing to be vulnerable.

Tom and I attended a conference where a father of an addict wisely encouraged us to develop the skill of discerning who could "carry our suitcase." This idea is from a story about a younger sister who overhears part of a conversation her father is having with her older sister about sex. She asks her dad when he will have this conversation with her, but he doesn't answer. Later, the younger sister and father are on an airplane. When they board the plane and get to their seats, the father asks her to reach up and put his suitcase in the overhead storage bin.

The daughter replies, "Daddy, I can't. Your suitcase is too heavy for me."

The father answers, "You're right, the suitcase is too heavy for you. I would never ask you to lift something that's too heavy and could hurt you. I love you and I'm asking you to trust me in the same way to have the sex talk with you when I think you can handle it."

For hurting parents, the suitcase symbolically holds the weight of our pain-filled story. Scary stuff. Not everyone can carry it. And that's okay. It's too heavy for most. But we only need a few people who can walk beside us to help us.

How do we approach potential suitcase carriers? What do we look for? Generally, don't approach a single person, couples without children, or parents of young children—they can't understand. Be cautious of those whose teen or adult children are high performers and achievers in their school or work. In addition, do your best to avoid people who talk too much, who tend to betray confidences. They may not be trustworthy.

Ask yourself if you think these people can carry the weight of your pain? Do you know if they've experienced much suffering themselves? What do they say about it? Are they grace-givers or more legalistic? This isn't a judgment on them but a recognition of their ability to enter into your suffering without invalidating it. In some cases you won't know until after you share some of your story. You'll have to be willing to risk a little to find out.

If they're aware you've been going through difficulties with your child, have they ever asked about them or shown much interest? You might ask if you could talk with them about it sometime, or you could invite them to have a cup of coffee with you to talk. In the beginning, reveal only a small amount of information. Notice how they respond. Are they shocked? Do they listen well and ask good questions? How did they make you feel? Guilty and embarrassed or at ease and comforted? Were they quick to give advice? If it was a positive experience, the next time you could share a little more and so on. Taking baby steps is probably a good rule of thumb to protect yourself from being hurt.

Ask God for a few suitcase carriers and for the gift of discernment to find them.

But please don't be too hard on those who can't share your burden.

It's not their fault. They simply aren't equipped for the job. Not now, anyway. But who knows, one day you might help carry theirs.

FACING YOUR GREATEST FEARS

When I was scared stiff for Reneé, I realized there was only one way to regain my sanity: face my fears head-on. For a long time they'd been too appalling even to think about. I stuffed all the what-if monsters deep inside. How could I confront and express them? Wouldn't facing them make them more real and cause me greater harm?

I decided to start by making a list of my fears by completing the following sentence: I am afraid because Reneé could . . .

- be kidnapped and held against her will
- be abducted and sold into sex trafficking; Orlando is one of the worst cities in the country for this problem
- disappear and never be seen or heard from again; we would have to live without ever knowing what happened
- move away, start a new life, and sever ties with us forever
- overdose and be in a vegetative state for the rest of her life
- suffer irreversible brain damage from her substance abuse
- die from alcohol poisoning
- die from an overdose
- get HIV or AIDS
- be murdered in a drug deal gone bad or because she was simply in the wrong place at the wrong time
- give up and commit suicide to end her suffering

Each one was possible and completely unacceptable to my heart.

One afternoon a dear friend invited me to her home to pray for our children. We spent several hours talking and reading the Scriptures. Finally, the moment came when God led her to ask, "Dena, what's your greatest fear for Reneé?" After a few minutes, I found the courage to say,

"I'm afraid she might die." Saying those words out loud opened the door to a time of weeping and lamenting over her.

Coming face to face with these dreadful yet possible outcomes and beginning to grieve my daughter's possible death was the most painful thing I've ever done. On my girlfriend's back porch on a warm spring afternoon, I finally accepted the reality that Reneé, my precious princess, could die. My nightmares could come true. One day I might have to identify her body in the morgue. I'd dreamed many times of doing that. I might have to choose her clothes for a viewing, plan her funeral, say good-bye, and never see her again in this life. She might never have a career, get married, or have a family. We would no longer have three children, but two. One of them would reside in heaven, arriving there before us. The death of a child is so unnatural, so unimaginable. If she died it would create a huge hole in our world for the rest of our lives.

I let myself feel the full weight of those possibilities and released the sorrow as much as I could. I cried torrents. When I did, God reassured me through His Word that if Reneé died, because of His unfailing love, He would never abandon me. I wouldn't be alone. Ever. Under any circumstances. He would be with me and He would help me.

Even if Reneé was never okay, I could be—because of Him. Somehow I would survive.

Let your fears draw you closer to the Lord. He offers comfort and reassurance to anyone who humbly comes to Him in faith, promising, "I am your God; I will strengthen you, I will help you, I will uphold you" (Isaiah 41:10, ESV).

Something remarkable occurred at my friend's house that day. Because I was willing to face my fears and start grieving the possibility of losing my daughter, the crippling torment of her possible death lost its power over me. My fears were disarmed and I was released.

Facing our fears strips them of their power in our lives and sets our hearts free.

How awesome is that? This is why I'm convinced we need to do the hard work of confronting those things we're afraid of. How could something so simple be so remarkable? Try it. Name your fears. Look directly at what might happen. And understand how close God is to the brokenhearted.

Here are two suggestions:

- **Give Yourself a Time Limit.** I set aside an amount of time to let myself worry. When I began to feel anxious, fearful, or worried, I would tell myself, I'm not going to think about that right now. I'll do that later, from 7:00 to 7:30 tonight. I made myself set those thoughts aside and wait. When the time came, I'd go to a solitary place where I could let myself fret and stew. I set an alarm and when it rang, I forced myself to stop—to mentally put those things away. It took a lot of self-control. I won't say I never worried at other times of the day, but I did it far less. It takes practice, but you can get better and better at it!

- **Make a God Box.** I learned to do this at an Al-Anon meeting. Take a small box and write My God Box on it. Put a small notepad and pen in it or beside it. When you realize you're worrying or feeling fearful, write those things on the notepad. Tear out the paper, fold it up, and put it in your box. Put the lid back on and put it away, maybe high on a shelf. It's the perfect symbol for acknowledging your fears, putting them into words, and giving them to God.

When we starve our fears and feed our faith, it brings about a shift of focus. Things start to change, not in our child necessarily, but in *us*. Fear begins to drain out. Peace inches back in. But be patient. It's a slow, gradual process.

There's plenty of help and hope for those who suffer with whatever our children are facing—if they'll accept it. A beautiful, productive life full of love and purpose is absolutely possible for your child and for you! We need to remind ourselves and our children of this often. They need all the encouragement and affirmation they can get. So do we.

God has a lot to say about fear and worry. He wants us to stop it. He doesn't want us to be tormented any longer. Bring it to Him. Let Him help you face your fears as you read His Word to see what it reveals. Spend time talking to Him in prayer. Take time to be still and let Him talk to you too. Prayer is a great healer.

His comfort is like no other. He can bring joy back into our lives again.

He wants you to remember what's true.

On our own, we can't do any of the things suggested in this chapter. But as Corrie ten Boom discovered in her suffering, when we come to Jesus for His help, *we can*. By His power and the Holy Spirit working in and through us, the impossible becomes possible. His strength, His ability, and His power miraculously become ours.

No matter what happens, Mom or Dad, God will be with you.

Scripture That Helps

But now, this is what the LORD says . . . : "Do not fear, for I have redeemed you; I have summoned you by name; you are mine. When you pass through the waters, I will be with you; and when you pass through the rivers, they will not sweep over you. When you walk through the fire, you will not be burned; the flames will not set you ablaze. For I am the LORD your God, the Holy One of Israel, your Savior. . . . Since you are precious and honored in my sight, and because I love you. . . . Do not be afraid, for I am with you." (Isaiah 43:1–5)

7

Grief and Loss

Pain will rip out whatever it can and destroy it. But smart parents will not let suffering take their spirit.

—William Coleman, *Parents with Broken Hearts*

*W*alking into the morgue, I knew Reneé's lifeless body lay beneath the stark white sheet. Stunned and alone, I was about to identify her body.

Kneeling beside a grave in the dark of night, I saw her name on the headstone, barely visible by the eerie light of the moon.

I couldn't stop crying, running from demons, my destruction their sole intention. An evil spirit, the shadow of death, stood at the foot of my bed. Waiting. Watching.

These were a few of the nightmares that plagued me. Sometimes I'd wake up sobbing and shaking, drenched in sweat. Other times I'd bolt up in bed and gasp for air.

Have you wondered how you would respond if any of your nightmares about your child came true? Do you think it would be the end of you, that you wouldn't be able to handle it? I've had conversations with many parents about this. Some don't know what they would do. Others say they'd run away or turn to a form of comfort (alcohol, prescription drugs, sex, food, television, sleep, shopping). A few said they might take the ultimate form of escape and end their lives.

Discovering your child is using drugs, has a drinking problem or same-sex attraction, is self-injuring, has an eating disorder or a mental illness or a brain disorder, is suicidal or made suicide attempts, is pregnant outside of marriage, was arrested, is incarcerated, has an addiction to pornography or any other heartbreaking, life-changing problem brings deep sadness. Maybe you've found yourself living in the middle of one of your nightmares.

GRIEF: AN UNEXPECTED RESPONSE

Did you know you were grieving? I didn't know I was. I first heard the concept related to the situations we face at a seminar for hurting parents. An experienced father of an addict told us that our feelings of sadness were a normal, healthy, emotional response to a significant loss. Grief wasn't only due to a death. He explained that we grieve when we lose a job, have financial problems, learn we have a health problem, lose a baby through miscarriage or a spouse through divorce, or when we have a child who struggles with potentially life-altering issues. Our beloved children have gone prodigal on us, and it feels like they died. Grief is a brutal, gut-wrenching, energy-sapping process that takes time to recover from. Everyone experiences it differently. But across the board, it affects every area of your life: emotional, physical, social, and spiritual.

As parents of troubled children, we're grieving a significant loss of the hopes we had for our kids. The recognition of those shattered dreams can be devastating. We feel pain and pressure on our chests as if a huge boulder were squashing us under its weight. My heart hurt from the relentless stress. Some days it felt as though it would burst. Does yours? During the day I repeatedly let out deep sighs as though they could release some of the pressure. I felt close to a breakdown most of the day and needed a Kleenex box nearby all the time.

How do you continue to work, manage finances, live your daily life, pursue family activities, and carry out your responsibilities? I had no idea. I was so lost. Attempts to follow my typical routine, even the spiritual disciplines that had helped in the past, failed. With poor focus and no energy or motivation, I couldn't do it. And I didn't care. My emotions flatlined as sadness overflowed. *It's my birthday? So what? Go on vacation? No way. Out to dinner with friends? Some other time.* It didn't feel right to have fun.

Conversations with a counselor helped some, but I still hadn't met anyone who could really understand my loss. Most of my friends had ideal families. *You're so lucky,* I'd think. *You haven't got a clue.* None were going through the kinds of things we were. I was so jealous. Envy began to gnaw at me. To my surprise, some of my closest friends pulled away. Our situation was too much. Is that your story?

Tension builds in your marriage. You don't always understand each other's responses, process your emotions the same way, or agree on what to do. You can't think about anything except your son or daughter. The strain does its damage. All your relationships suffer. Your health might too. Struggling with a digestive disorder that flares up under stress, I lost twenty pounds in two months. That's not how you want to lose weight.

Grief can be crushing. While you're out running errands, you hope you don't see anyone you know. The last thing you want to hear is, "How's your son or daughter doing?" *Please, please don't ask. And don't tell me how great your child's doing either or about their college plans, degrees, job, engagement, or marriage.* You can't take it. You might not have heard from your child in months or years. I wanted to be invisible.

You wonder if you'll ever laugh again. When will you be able to get through the day without humiliating yourself in front of strangers, crying at the most unexpected times? What happened to the child you once knew? Where did they go? You want them back.

How can you ever be the same?

You can't.

TRIGGERS: WHAT JUMP-STARTS THE PAIN

During the time when I couldn't talk about my daughter's issues—especially the rapes—tears flowed freely whenever I encountered something called a *trigger*. Triggers are places, situations, or anything that evokes painful feelings, in this case, all we've lost with our child. They're reminders, moments that sneak up on us and take us by surprise. One mom calls them emotional ambushes. Encountering a trigger would cause me to lose my composure in public places when I was trying my best to be brave. I didn't want to show the depth of my pain to people I didn't know, at least not very well. It was too personal.

You probably have triggers too. Learn what they are. My list might help you identify a few of yours:

- Happy families with little girls or boys, especially if they reminded me of my daughter. I wanted to beg the parents to protect their children with great care, to lock them in their rooms until they were thirty, to enjoy every moment with them now before their son or daughter hated them.

- Pregnant women. I wanted to warn them that they didn't know what heartache could be ahead.

- Certain types of music or songs, especially during worship at church.

- Sporting events or other activities Reneé had participated in.

- A scene in a movie or television program about the issues I was dealing with.

- Jokes that made light of the issues.

- The routine question most cashiers happily ask, "How are you?" Many times I almost screamed back, "Terrible! I don't know where my daughter is. She's killing herself with drugs and alcohol. I may never see her alive again!"

- Going to restaurants or social events that offered alcoholic beverages.
- Places I'd previously gone to and enjoyed with my child: the beach, a park, a restaurant.
- Anything that prompted a thought or memory of Reneé.

Identifying your triggers may take a while, but when you learn to recognize them, it will help prevent you from being caught by surprise as often. But the nature of triggers is that you can't always see them coming. You can, however, prepare yourself somewhat by anticipating a difficult situation ahead of time. You might decide not to put yourself in that situation or you might plan an escape. Politely decline the invitation to a graduation open house, a bridal or baby shower, even a wedding. Give yourself permission in advance that it's okay to excuse yourself and leave if you feel your emotions building. Take deep, cleansing breaths to calm down and slow your pulse. Plan your response to uncomfortable questions you know might be coming:

"How is Susie doing?" *"She's fine. How's your daughter?"*

"What college did Tim get into?" *"He's doing something else right now. How is your son doing in school?"*

"How have you been lately?" *"I'm okay. What have you been up to?"*

An effective strategy is to ask them a question to turn the focus back on them as soon as possible. You're under no obligation to tell anyone about your child's private life. These things can help us maintain our emotional stability a little better during a difficult time in our lives.

A Unique Grief: Sexual Assault

My greatest sadness was when I found out my daughter had been raped—more than once. Sexual assault of a child is a unique kind of grief. Engulfed in deep sorrow, I thought, *Oh, God, no, no, no.* The pain was excruciating. How could I survive this? How could she? Has this happened to you? Did you ask yourself these same questions? Turning to God's Word I read, "And the God of all grace . . . after you have suffered a little while, will himself restore you and make you strong, firm, and steadfast" (1 Peter 5:10). I hoped this was true.

Sadly, sexual assault is a common crime against addicts, and not just women, either. Drunk or high, they're vulnerable targets. In some ways, slashing and tearing at their flesh is an understandable reaction. Rape is the ultimate degradation. *Who will want me now?* they think. *I'm just used goods.* Disgraced and humiliated, they no longer feel worthy of life or love or anything good. They conclude that death would be a welcome relief. No wonder so many take their lives. *God, have mercy.*

Words are insufficient to describe the intensity of this pain to a parent's soul. If you've been through it with your child, you know what it's like. It cuts deep furrows into your soul. It burns and pummels and debilitates where no eye can see. There aren't enough tears. Nothing else felt so devastating or brought so much brokenness. Any previous anguish on my journey couldn't compare. For many parents, sexual molestation of their children is the supreme wound to their hearts.

Fathers whose daughters have been sexually assaulted are especially tormented. Their hearts throb with a profound sense of loss. They're inconsolable over the reality that they couldn't protect their little girls, couldn't keep them safe. No number of butterfly kisses can make it all better or take their hurt away. Rage fills them with a desire for revenge and justice. Not many get the restitution they deserve. If that's you, I'm so sorry.

Whatever the cause is of the despair we feel over our children, we have lots of unanswered questions. Why didn't God protect them? Was He too busy solving the problems of the world? We don't understand. He doesn't seem very loving and good anymore. Why did we bother to pray? It didn't make any difference.

Can these wounds heal? Will we ever recover from this mortal blow? Is it possible to enjoy anything again? We're undone. We feel as though we've been shattered into a million little pieces.

Learning about a rape can take you to a very dark place. It did for me. I wanted to die.

What was your darkest moment? Your greatest pain and heartache you've grieved over? Did you long for death? I thought it would have been easier. Then I wouldn't have to experience this wretched agony. What about you?

Where can we go to escape our suffering? How can we heal the damage inflicted on our hearts and souls? How can we cope with the misery? How can we process our feelings? I had no clue. I didn't know what I felt other than an indescribable woe that was too awful to put into words. "Indeed, we felt we had received the sentence of death," Paul wrote (2 Corinthians 1:9). Discovering the depths of Reneé's troubles plummeted me to a new phase of my journey—deep grief.

PROFESSIONAL AID

Not sure you need help processing your grief? Look for these symptoms in yourself or in your child:
- frequent nightmares
- overwhelming sadness
- an obsession with the loss or traumatic event
- loss of appetite
- crying spells
- nervousness and high anxiety
- insomnia
- sleeping too much
- inability to concentrate
- memory loss and forgetfulness
- overeating

- agitation over little things with increasing episodes of anger
- numerous physical ailments, such as headaches, stomach problems, and nausea

These may be intensified in cases of a sexual assault.

Tom and I had many of these symptoms. If you recognize more than a few of them in yourself, you could probably benefit from professional help, especially if your symptoms last more than a month. It can't hurt. Some counselors will talk with you on the phone to determine whether or not a few sessions would be beneficial for you.

We looked online for a support group that could help us process our feelings. That's when we found Al-Anon. We also found a therapist-led group just for parents whose children had been victims of sexual assault. We were desperate for help, knowing we couldn't get through this on our own. Desperation gave us the courage we needed to participate in these groups. We attended the one for sexual abuse every week for a year. That group became a vital part of our healing journey. It helped us identify our feelings, face them, talk about them, and process them with others who were going through the same thing. It also helped us understand what our daughter was going through.

In this safe, caring community, we expressed our rage in healthy ways. We revealed our fears for her future, of her possibly contracting HIV or AIDS. We made posters and painted T-shirts that we shared with each other in the group, showing how we felt before and after the assaults. We shared our recovery goals and held each other accountable. We cheered each other on, celebrating every small victory. We admitted our desire for the rapists to suffer as our children had, even to pay the highest price for their crime—with their lives. Some in our group filed criminal charges. We supported them on that treacherous path. How powerful to share in each other's recovery.

Through participating in this therapeutic group, Tom and I found the help we needed. We shared a long, grueling journey together from grief and hate to peace and forgiveness. It brought us great healing.

You, too, can experience this as you grieve the losses with your child. If you have the need, I urge you to find a therapist or support group near you today. There are groups for people with loved ones who suffer from most any kind of life-altering illness or addiction (see the resource section at the back of the book).

Reneé: On Handling Your Child's Pain After a Sexual Assault

It's okay to express anger as long as it's not at your children. Openly placing blame on them is not helpful, especially in response to a sexual assault. You have to ask God for wisdom to know what your children need. It may be healthy for them to see your reaction, to see you process it. That may help validate what they're feeling. Show your grief. Your children may not know how to feel about what is happening to them.

Learn about posttraumatic stress disorder (PTSD) so you can be aware of the symptoms and get professional help for your children and so you can be gracious and understanding about how your children may be acting. Be sensitive to their triggers and really, really emphasize that they need help. If they don't have therapy to process the pain, it will affect them for years. Inform yourself and become aware.

You can't fix or solve their problems, but you can do your best to understand them for your own healing. Be aware of the different ways they may respond, and don't take it personally. They may say no to a bunch of things now, since their no didn't matter at the time of the sexual assault. They may say no to the smallest and most random things: to things they used to like or to things you or their friends ask them to do. I just remember that *no* was the most important word to me in the

THE BALM OF PRAYER

Something else that helped me process my grief was to spend time with people who were gifted in praying. I call them my prayer warriors.[11] I found them by seeking help from the staff at my church and through

world for a really long time. I would say no to hanging out, helping with something, riding in a car with someone or going somewhere, letting someone borrow something or using something of theirs—any situation where I felt I wasn't in control. For your child it could be to something you ask them, such as "Do you want to do this?" "Would you like a slice of pizza?" "Do you want to watch this movie?" It's pretty vague sounding, but it was a big thing for me and many other survivors.

They may become unreasonably angry and agitated by people, things, situations, sounds, smells, colors, places, songs, touch, certain words, or topics of conversation. They may blow up at you for what seems to be a completely normal question or statement, but the phrasing or feeling it creates may cause flashbacks and remind them of the incident. They may be quick to pass judgment on others, speak hatefully or defensively when triggering people or situations come up. They might become apathetic. They might desensitize themselves by binge watching crime shows and movies or reading books that show people being brutalized, going through the same trauma they went through. This can fluctuate or range from one end of the spectrum to the other. This is part of PTSD.

Don't force them to talk about what happened. Any sense of a loss of control afterward is even more traumatic. They need to feel in control, to know their voice is important, that it matters. They need a safe place to feel whatever they're feeling and have permission to express it so they can fully heal.

friends. They became some of my suitcase carriers. They helped me draw closer to wholeness. During our times together, God met me in meaningful ways and showed His love, understanding, and compassion. They wept with me and sat with me in my pain. When my faith was weak, they offered faith-filled requests on my behalf. They brought Reneé and me to the throne of God when I was too weighed down to go on my own, interceding for both of us. Prayer became another powerful vehicle for deep, inner healing. God used its powerful effects to help me not let suffering take my spirit. Through the beauty and profound supernatural mystery of prayer, He protected my bruised heart and soul. Scripture says, "Out of my distress I called on the LORD; the LORD answered me and set me free" (Psalm 118:5, ESV).

As you grieve, remember to be patient with yourself. It may take a long time to process your feelings about what's happened to your child as well as the sadness over the other losses you've encountered. You're normal. These are significant losses. It's taken me years, and I'm still working on it. Here's a reality check. Even though you've experienced huge amounts of deep, inner healing, you may always carry an ache in your heart over your child's suffering. That's normal too. But it's possible to make peace with the pain. By God's grace, you can find freedom from the torment and not let it rob you of your own life. You and I can even forgive those who took advantage of our children (we'll take a look at the topic of forgiveness in the next chapter).

How to Not Let Suffering Take Your Spirit

When we discover our precious children have been affected by a host of troubling, destructive behaviors, it can have the same impact as though they had died (their age doesn't matter). They will never be the same and neither will we, but we can feel whole again. Enjoy life again. Not let it destroy us.

The opening quote for this chapter urges us to "not let suffering take [your] spirit." If you do these things, with God's help, it won't:

- Accept that your pain is real and you're grieving. Don't minimize it. In the suffering you've been through with your child, you've lost something significant and important and can never get it back. Your life has been altered.

- Give yourself permission to be real about your suffering, to feel the pain. You can't avoid it. Don't stuff it, deny it, or try to escape from it by sleeping a lot or self-medicating. This can make you sick and lengthen the grieving process. Distractions are okay for a little while, such as working longer hours, staying busy, eating comfort foods, taking naps, exercising more, shopping. But be careful not to overdo it.

- Find healthy ways to express your hurt. Whatever you're feeling is okay, whether it's anger, numbness, guilt, shame, sadness, or any other emotion. Don't let others tell you how you should feel. Talk to a trusted friend, journal if you like to write, paint if you're an artist, take up kickboxing, or play music. Find a healthy way to release these negative emotions.

- Be thankful for today and don't look too far ahead. This only causes more fear and anxiety. You can cope with right now, and that's all you have to do. Stay in the present. Start a gratitude list and add to it daily. Notice little things. Enjoy one moment at a time. Rejoice in small victories.

- Admit your need for help. Search the Internet, call counselors, clergy, churches, police departments, or the local hospital until you find what you need. Your community has resources and can assist you and your child.

- Adjust to the new normal. Shift your focus to healthy activities. Try to keep doing typical daily tasks.

- Simplify as much as possible. Less activity is best for a season. You need to conserve your energy just to survive.
- Take care of yourself. You deserve a lot of TLC right now. Eat healthfully, get adequate rest, drink lots of water, try to exercise at least fifteen to thirty minutes three times per week, and take a nap when needed if you can.
- Don't let your child become the sole focus of your world. Look for someone else in need. Send a card or an e-mail, take flowers or a meal, invite the person out for coffee, or make a phone call. Getting your mind off yourself and your problems is always a good thing. "As we have opportunity," Scripture says, "let us do good to all people" (Galatians 6:10).
- Trust God with what you can't understand. As much as you want to, you don't need to know why things happen the way they do. Choose to rest in a sovereign, loving Creator, and be content with not knowing how He can use it for good in your life.
- Most of all, remember: *You are not alone.* You can't hear this enough. God, our heavenly Father, will never, ever abandon you. He understands your grief and loss. He cares. He weeps with you. You can count on Him to keep His promises.

The people I know with the strongest faith are those who've suffered most yet never turned away from God. They dug in deeper. One of them made this comment to me during a recent visit: "These last five years in my battle with cancer, as much as I would never have wanted it, I can honestly say that as a result, my faith has grown richer and sweeter. I wouldn't trade that for anything in the world."

It was rough when I accepted the losses, left denial behind, processed the shock, began to cope with anger, and faced my fears. I had to do a lot of hard work. But it all helped. The pain of grief can rip through your life and destroy you. Choose to start taking steps for your healing today. Instead of running away from God, run to Him, dig in deeper, then suffering won't take your spirit.

Scripture That Helps

The LORD is close to the brokenhearted and saves those who are crushed in spirit. (Psalm 34:18)

You, Lord, are forgiving and good, abounding in love to all who call to you. (Psalm 86:5)

8

Forgiveness

Forgiveness can only emerge from great strength of soul.
It is a clear sign of the courageous, humble resilience of the
human spirit undergirded by grace.

—Marjorie J. Thompson, *The Way of Forgiveness*

When Reneé moved out after a traumatic event, hurt, anger, and bitterness moved in—to my heart. How could my own child reject and hurt me this way? How could I forgive her?

Truth be told, our sons and daughters may not know they need forgiving. They've made choices that hurt us and cost us: our health, our sleep, our work, our finances (spent trying to help them or ourselves), our mental and emotional well-being, and our relationships with them, our spouses, other children, family members, and friends. Our faith may even have been weakened. We may have walked away from God in disillusionment and confusion. Asking forgiveness probably isn't our children's focus; eliminating their pain is.

But forgiveness isn't just for the person who needs to be forgiven. It also benefits the forgivers—you and me. It doesn't make the other person right, but it makes us free. One of my recovery support group meeting leaders explained, "Forgiveness doesn't condone or excuse behavior. It releases our loved one to let God deal with him or her." For parents in pain, forgiveness is part of the process of getting back our lives. Therefore we need to forgive for the sake of our own souls.

One day my friend Judy Douglass sent me an e-mail about the challenge to forgive her son:

> I still remember the night he lied to me on his way to spend the night with his girlfriend.
>
> The terrible things he said to me in his great drunkenness. The night he and his high friends frightened our houseguest into her room. And when he stole from his sister. The lies, the drinking and drugs, the stealing—they happened a lot. There were consequences, but there was also God-given grace and mercy.
>
> But those specific events—they have been harder. I have forgiven them many times. I put them behind me and moved on in peace. But then something triggers a memory, the pain resurfaces, the anger returns. And once again I need to consciously extend mercy—I need to forgive. He, of course, knows nothing of [my] ongoing battle over [his] past offenses.
>
> Unforgiveness is exhausting. Eventually our prodigals need to know they are forgiven for all they have done—though usually that need comes after they have made some kind of turnaround.
>
> When we are not able to forgive, we are the ones who are being worn out and worn down.
>
> We must forgive them—and in that we will find rest.

We need that rest. M. Scott Peck observed, "If we hold on to our anger, we stop growing and our souls begin to shrivel."[12] When our children inflict wounds on our hearts—with vicious words, valuables that disappeared, broken promises, values and beliefs rejected, and countless other offenses—we grieve the loss of the hopes and dreams we had for them, their futures, and the relationships we longed for.

But weary parent, what's done is done. We need to let go of what we can.

I know this doesn't sound hopeful, but it's realistic.

The Excuses We Make

Forgiving our children can be complicated. We've become pretty good at making excuses for them. Recognize any of these?

- "He didn't really mean it."
- "She couldn't help it."
- "He had too much to drink. It wasn't his fault."
- "She didn't know what she was doing."
- "She wouldn't do that if she knew how much it hurt me."
- "His friends are making him do these things."

Sooner or later, however, we need to realize our children are responsible for how they've hurt us. It doesn't matter if they meant to or not. And we're responsible for forgiving them. I resonate with what David Augsburger noted: "We forgive . . . when we hold [others] accountable but do not excuse."[13]

We've covered for our children and explained away their hurtful actions long enough. To be brutally honest, it's possible to not even like them as they are now. "I'm ashamed to admit this, but I don't even want to be around my son anymore. I can't stand him. Sometimes I hate him, the person he's become. I don't know who he is anymore," a mom confided to me. Don't be embarrassed. Admit it, bring it to the Lord in prayer, and when you feel ready, move on to extend mercy and forgiveness.

Please don't misunderstand. I don't mean to tell you to do this today. You might not be ready. You can't hurry the process. Give yourself time to feel your feelings first. Eventually we need to face our hurts so we can leave them behind or they'll consume us. Admit them to yourself, acknowledge the ways you've been hurt. It helped me to write Reneé a letter telling her all the ways she had done that to me. I ranted and raved and put it all out there. And then I destroyed the letter. Getting those feelings out, seeing them on paper and in black and white had a therapeutic effect. Held inside, they'll make us miserable. But it's our choice.

FIVE AREAS OF FORGIVENESS

On our own we can't forgive, at least I couldn't. We need our Redeemer, the Master Forgiver, to show us the way. He gave us the best example to follow. He repeatedly offered forgiveness to His wayward people in the Old Testament and then through His Son, Jesus. The apostle Paul wrote, "Bear with each other and forgive one another. . . . Forgive as the Lord forgave you" (Colossians 3:13). Our Savior forgave those who crucified Him in the midst of His suffering. What an example. Through His saving work on the cross, all our sins have been forgiven. He's removed them from us as far as the east is from the west. How can we not follow in His steps by offering forgiveness? If we don't, our unforgiveness will only hurt us in the end.

Here are five areas in which we need to practice the fine art of forgiveness.

1. We Need to Forgive Our Children for How They Hurt Us

We may be furious and resentful over how we've been treated. They lied to us, stole from us, and subjected us to verbal abuse: "I hate you." "You ruined my life." "I can't wait to get away from you, %*@!#." Some have been physically abusive. The list goes on. We can't trust them alone in our own homes. We can't believe anything they say. We don't even know who they are anymore. They've broken our hearts and trashed our dreams, but we must forgive them even if they don't ask us to. We don't do it based on our feelings—that might never happen—but by faith and out of love for the Lord and for them. Forgiving is an act of our will and a desire to do what we believe is pleasing to God. When we step out in simple obedience, it's a strange thing how our feelings can begin to change. Not overnight, but over time something begins to shift deep inside of us. Forgiving again and again, each time hurt and anger rise up, protects us from becoming bitter. Sooner or later, we realize that we really *can* forgive. "Forgive, and you will be forgiven," the Lord said (Luke 6:37).

2. We Need to Forgive Ourselves for Our Mistakes

Even though we did our best, sometimes we still feel guilty over any part we may have played in our children's issues. We beat ourselves up over what we didn't see or what we allowed. Why weren't we stronger or smarter? We need to be kind to ourselves and refuse the lies the devil, our enemy, wants us to believe. He wants to destroy our faith, our marriages, our families, and our children. Remember the three statements I encouraged you to write on an index card in chapter 2? I hope you did so that you see them often. Here they are again: *You are not alone. You are not a bad parent. You are going to be okay.* It's the truth.

Think about it. We never forced our children to drink, take drugs, break the law, or do any of the dangerous, abusive, foolish, criminal things they've done. We didn't cause them to have mental health issues, either, although some of them are genetic. For example, bipolar disorder tends to run in families. My mother struggled with this most of her life. I had to alleviate myself of any guilt by accepting the fact that passing this on to Reneé was beyond my control. I wasn't to blame. I didn't decide to do this to her. Therefore I needed to stop being so hard on myself about it anymore than if she'd inherited some other physical disease from my side of the gene pool. These things happen. Of course we feel bad, but it's time to stop beating ourselves up over them.

We all did the best we could and we all made mistakes. No matter how much we may have blown it, our children are responsible for their choices. God gave them a free will to make their own decisions. Don't forget what happened in the Garden of Eden to the only perfect parent (Genesis 2). Forgive yourself or you will suffer the heavy weight of guilt, blame, and shame God never intended for you to carry.

3. We Need to Forgive Others for How They Hurt Our Children

We need to forgive the people who were bad influences, who encouraged their destructive choices, who sold or gave them drugs, who partied with them, who committed crimes with them, who exposed them to pornography, who abused them, took advantage of them, or didn't help them when they could have. They're tough to forgive, but if we don't, bitterness, hatred, and a desire for revenge can take root in our hearts. Remember, forgiveness isn't saying "What you did was okay." Forgiveness is choosing to let go of the anger and pain you've held on to; it's choosing to not let that person have any control over your emotions any longer.

4. We Need to Forgive Those Who Hurt Us

These are the family members, friends, and coworkers who didn't mean to, but they caused us pain. A disapproving look or a thoughtless remark based on ignorance or pride. They meant well. Some offered advice that felt more like a slap in the face. They made attempts to explain, but they only made us feel worse. They couldn't understand, didn't know what to do, said the wrong thing, looked down on us, or walked away. It wasn't their fault. They didn't know any better. Don't hold it against them. You could be resentful, but remember, there may be times you unintentionally hurt someone too. You didn't know any better, either. Do you want to be forgiven?

5. We Need to Forgive God

Does it sound strange that we need to forgive God? It's challenging to accept that God—who is sovereign, almighty, wise, loving, and good—could have prevented these things, yet He gave our children the right to make their own choices. Sometimes we blame God for not protecting them from temptation and harm. We rail against Him for allowing terrible things to happen, though much of our children's trauma is the natural consequence of their poor decisions.

Of course, God doesn't need to be forgiven. He didn't do anything wrong. In reality, we're the ones who need to be forgiven if we've begun to blame Him, allowing resentment to build up in our hearts without realizing it. And we can become cynical. That only hurts us. The important thing is to be honest and tell Him what we're feeling. It's okay. He understands. He gets it. He gets us.

One morning during a time of personal prayer I realized I was blaming God. *Lord, I know it wasn't really Your fault. You didn't choose to hurt me. But for my own good I need to tell You that I forgive You for allowing Reneé to make countless horrific choices, for the terrible things that happened to her as a result, for permitting her to struggle with a brain disorder and letting me experience all this pain. I don't think I'll ever understand, but I can't hold on to unforgiveness. I have to release it.*

"The first and only person to be healed by forgiveness," says one of my friends, "is the person who does the forgiveness. 'When we forgive, we set a prisoner free and discover that the prisoner we set free is us.'"[14]

This business of forgiving is tough. How can we do this hard thing? By choosing to do so. I believe it's an act of our will, like choosing to love someone who's not easy to love. We forgive by faith not feelings. Is that hypocritical? I don't think so. We do a lot of things we don't feel like doing because we know it's the right thing to do. But don't push yourself before you think you're ready. Give yourself the space you need to process what you've been through. Forgiveness can't be on anyone else's timetable but your own.

The biggest thing that helped me even want to attempt to forgive was to remind myself how much God had forgiven me. Did Jesus feel like forgiving when He hung on the cross, as Joni Eareckson Tada described, "like meat on a stick"? Maybe not, yet He did. Therefore He's the perfect one to help you and me. We can forgive those who don't deserve it because He forgave us. You may have been a Christian a long time. You've heard this before—you know it well—but acting on it in the situation you're in is another thing altogether, isn't it?

A refusal to forgive is a serious thing. It can bring consequences to our health and overall well-being. We need to offer and receive forgiveness more than we realize. If we don't, it can lead to bitterness, resentment, and cynicism. None of which is good. Forgiveness is the only way to lance our heart wounds before they fester and make us sick. Soul sick.

Jesus is our role model. He's the how and the why of forgiving. Like grieving, forgiving is a long, slow process, but if we choose to take this path—the path less traveled—we can find freedom.

WE NEED FORGIVENESS TOO

We need not only to forgive others, but we need to ask forgiveness *from* our children for our mistakes. We may or may not have known God and His ways in the years we were raising them. Even if we did, we're still human. We all made at least a few errors. For some of us it was more than a few. When we humble ourselves, admit we blew it at times, and ask their forgiveness, we can find a lot of relief and healing. And it takes the pressure off our children to be flawlessly good to earn our approval. And that's a really great thing.

If God reveals a time you messed up or unintentionally hurt your child by being too harsh or too lenient, by causing an offense, or by en-abling, admit your failure and ask your child to forgive you. This act of humility can have huge benefits for your relationship. There's no guarantee, but if God leads you to ask them for forgiveness, trust Him with the results. Allison Bottke, a mom who understands, said, "This crucial step of asking the forgiveness of your adult child, though very hard, may be the healing balm needed to prepare him or her for an enhanced growth spurt."[15]

But what if your child isn't ready to forgive, reacts badly, launches into more blaming, and starts listing additional offenses, such as "You did this and you did that!" As much as it hurts, the best response is to tell them, "I'm really sorry you feel that way. You have a right to your feelings, the same as I do. I hope someday you can forgive me so our relationship can be better."

Don't let them put false guilt on you. Try to understand it might be their addiction or mental illness talking, or they may not be able to respond rationally for a number of other possible reasons. Could it be that they need you to be the bad guy so they can feel better about themselves? Nevertheless, continue to offer forgiveness as you politely remove yourself from the situation. Nothing good will come from further conversation. It's likely to deteriorate into an argument. Tell them you love them and calmly walk away.

Pain Won't Last

Helplessly standing by, watching our children ruin their lives is dreadful. When they reject us, push us away, wound us, and walk out of our lives, they probably aren't really rejecting us or our love, but rather our values, beliefs, and boundaries. When God and family and friends let us down, the pain cuts deep. For some of you, your pain may never end. You'll have to accept that, make peace with it, give it to God, and go on with your life without a peaceful resolution. I'm so sorry. But you can know with certainty that He won't waste one moment of your heartache. He'll use all of it to change you, grow you stronger, bring you closer to Him, and help others. Because of what you've been through, you can know the Creator of the universe in far deeper ways than you ever thought possible. In addition, you can bring Him glory—if you let Him use your pain for good. You can be sure He will. And I promise you, the pain won't last forever, even though it feels like it will. It's temporary.

One day it will come to an end, if not in this life, then in the next, when you reach your heavenly home. You might be thinking this isn't very comforting right now, but in the midst of the chaos, it helps to have realistic expectations and an eternal perspective. That's what I want for you, not pie-in-the-sky, Pollyanna hope. Like you, I had to face reality. I don't want to offer false hope or say what you want to hear just to make

Reneé:
On Forgiveness

I remember seeing my parents for the first time after I had entered treatment. There was this huge knot in my throat, and I could feel the tears welling up. I felt like a little child who just woke up from a nightmare, soothed and comforted almost instantly just by the sight of their parents. Or that feeling when you slam your knees into the concrete, and the moment your mom or dad comes to hold you until the shock wears off. You collapse in their arms in a sobbing heap. Anyway, I remember the first thing out of my mouth was an apology. I felt their unconditional love for me, the haze had lifted, and all of the devastation I had caused was so agonizingly clear.

I could see the mixture of pain and love and relief in their eyes, and I was so sorry I had ever hurt their hearts. Flashbacks of gut-wrenching moments burst through my mind. I could see my parents sitting in emergency rooms, visiting me in psych wards. I imagined my mother's sweet soul aching late into the night as she prayed through her tears, the way my father's eyes looked when he saw my self-inflicted wounds, and my heart broke for them—but not in a punishing way. I allowed myself to feel what they must have felt, to empathize with them, and I was overwhelmed with gratitude for their relentless love and hope they had for me. Later, in one of the family groups, we were able to start the process of forgiveness. Each of us took a turn to speak and listen, to share our hurts and acknowledge each other's pain and apologize for our part. It was a beautiful, vulnerable act of transparency that provided an opportunity for love to be present and healing to begin.

you feel better. That would only create bigger problems down the road for you.

Remember, instead, God understands our hurt far more than we can imagine. He's the ultimate rejected, offended, brokenhearted parent. His heart's been crushed millions and millions of times. In a very real way we share in His sufferings. Ours pales by comparison, but we've entered into the pain of the Father of all mankind. Jesus bore this agony when He died on the cross for every person who has lived or is yet to be born.

But how wonderful to know that as we share in His pain, we also share in His reassuring comfort: "For just as we share abundantly in the sufferings of Christ, so also our comfort abounds through Christ" (2 Corinthians 1:5). Now that's a promise we can hold on to.

Remember, we can't change what's happened. Stop trying. Let's focus on ourselves instead. That's hard enough. When we ask God for help, He'll empower us to forgive even those who committed unthinkable crimes against our children. In Him, forgiveness becomes possible. We can leave our sons and daughters in His hands. He's got them.

Scripture That Helps

When I said, "My foot is slipping," your unfailing love, LORD, supported me. When anxiety was great within me, your consolation brought me joy. (Psalm 94:18–19)

The LORD is a refuge for the oppressed, a stronghold in times of trouble. Those who know your name trust in you, for you, LORD, have never forsaken those who seek you. (Psalm 9:9–10)

9

Letting Go

But we have this treasure in jars of clay to show that this
all-surpassing power is from God and not from us. We are
hard pressed on every side, but not crushed; perplexed, but
not in despair.

—2 Corinthians 4:7-8

In the story *Alice's Adventures in Wonderland,* a young girl falls into a
foreign world full of unexpected twists and turns she can't escape.
That's how I felt on my painful parenting journey: lost and powerless.

After Reneé's two stints in a local behavioral hospital following episodes of severe cutting and suicidal ideation, Tom and I shamelessly
begged her to enter a ninety-day rehab. "If you'll find a place, I'll go," she
consented. Overjoyed, we were full of hope that this was *it.*

*Maybe she's finally ready to be done. Could this be what we've been
waiting for?* We were sure it was.

We threw ourselves into finding the perfect program. But there
wasn't one. They all have strengths and weaknesses. It's good to know
this in advance. I wish someone had told me ahead of time so I would've
had more realistic expectations. Her dad spent hours searching the Internet, making calls, talking endlessly to intake personnel until his ears were
sore. Now we know we should've let Reneé take ownership in the process
and do the work herself. But we couldn't let go yet.

It's best to get your child involved. If it's their first time going to rehab, you could narrow it down to a few programs for them to consider, especially if they also struggle with mental illness. The process is very time consuming and could easily overwhelm them. Let them do as much as you think they can handle. You may not know what that is until you let them try. If you have insurance that will pay part of the cost, you'll need to give them that information to help narrow their choices. Encourage them to look over the websites, make a list of questions, then call and talk to an intake or admissions counselor (this is eventually required before acceptance anyway). If they've been in rehab before, they know how it works.

Your son or daughter may be very appreciative that you let them choose where they want to go. If they're too sick, encourage their involvement as much as possible. If they're too lazy and want you to do all the work, be strong and say, "You know what? In spite of all you've been through, I'm confident you'll find the place that's right for you. I don't mind helping you some, but you need to do what you can. Do your best and let me know if you need any assistance, but the decision is yours."

Even if they're in jail, inmates are allowed to make these types of phone calls. They have caseworkers who help by suggesting local programs. They're well acquainted with them. Overall, the more your child's in the driver's seat with the decision-making process, the more invested they'll be when they go into the program. It's also a good way to determine how motivated for change they really are. This is for their life and their future—no one else's. Recovery is hard work, and rehabs are ridiculously expensive. Therefore they need to be ready to take it seriously.

We found a faith-based program in South Florida that sounded good. Preparations were made for Reneé to stay three months and then go into their halfway house. We were thrilled. After all, how much worse could it get? Hadn't she endured enough bad experiences to want a better life? Now the choice was hers. Would she work the steps of a recovery program? We hoped so. Would she stay the whole ninety days? We wanted her to, but she could leave at any time. No one could keep her there. Would she learn what she needed to stay clean and live in a whole new way? Time would tell. It was all up to her. No one can force another person to be ready to be *done* with their substance abuse or any other harmful behavior. They're the only ones who have any control over their recovery. Period.

LEARNING FROM RELAPSE

Reneé did go to rehab. She completed ninety days and spent about a month in a halfway house. She seemed better and healthier every time we saw her on family weekends.

One night when Reneé was walking back to the halfway house with a fellow resident, three men in ski masks attacked and robbed her. Traumatized, with head and neck injuries, she returned home with our blessing, never to return to the program. We prayed the trauma wouldn't trigger a relapse. However, unknown to anyone, a setback had already begun.

Our daughter's counselor told us, "When Reneé leaves our program, she won't be the same person. Even if she relapses, she'll never be like she was before coming here. She's going to learn everything she needs to know and will have all the tools necessary to get clean and stay clean if she wants to."

Upon hearing that, I prayed, *Oh, God, please don't let her relapse— ever. I don't think I could take it. I need her to be okay so I can be okay.*

After being back in Orlando a few days, one evening Reneé went to a party. We were on pins and needles. Later that night, she called. "Hey, Dad, I just wanted to let you guys know I'm going to spend the night with my girlfriend."

"Oh? Well, okay," Tom said, full of apprehension. "But I have to ask you a question. Is this because you're having such a good time or because you've been drinking and you plan on drinking more?"

With a calm sadness in her voice, she responded, "I've been drinking."

"Well, then, you know what that means. We talked about this when you returned from rehab. Choosing to drink means you're choosing to live somewhere else. We can't do this again."

We'd laid out clear boundaries. Everyone understood. Tom and I would support her recovery and sobriety efforts 100 percent, but we weren't going to enable her to use under our roof. There would be zero tolerance for touching alcohol or drugs. We refused to help her destroy herself.

"I know, Dad. I'll be by to pick up my things sometime tomorrow afternoon. Okay?"

We couldn't sleep that night. Our emotions were all over the map— anger, sadness, fear, and shock. We were so distraught, the tears wouldn't stop flowing. *How could she do this?* we asked ourselves. *After all we've done for her? After all she's learned? What is she thinking? Doesn't she realize how dangerous this is? Where will this lead?*

Mom, Dad, have you been through this with your son or daughter? If so, you've tasted the devastation of this kind of disappointment, of having a relapsed child. You know how it knocks the wind out of you, blindsides you, and wipes you out. Or did you see it coming and have a sense something was wrong?

In recovery meetings we learned that relapse never comes without warning. There are indicators that alert you that something's amiss. Here are several common warning signs to look for:

- They stop going to recovery meetings and/or meeting with their sponsor—or they never get a sponsor. They no longer do the things they were doing to help them stay strong. They make excuses for not doing them. "I'm too tired." "I forgot." "I didn't feel like it." "People weren't friendly to me." "Someone was mean to me." "It's just one time." "It's not a big deal." "I'll go tomorrow." "I don't feel safe there." "Those people are crazy." "It's not helping me that much anyway." "I don't really need that anymore." "I already know all those things."

- They become moody, selfish, and ungrateful again. Bad attitudes and old behavior patterns return. They spend too much time alone in their room and react very defensively when asked about it.

- They complain and feel sorry for themselves a lot. "I don't have a car (or a driver's license) anymore." "I can't find a job." "No one's going to hire me." "It's so difficult to get rides to meetings." "No one wants to help me." "This is too hard."

- They don't accept responsibility for the consequences of their actions and blame others for their problems. "If you wouldn't have . . ." "I have this problem because they . . ." "I can't do _____ because _____ did _____. This isn't my fault." "It's not fair."

- They begin to reconnect with old friends who aren't a good influence or go back to former hangouts. They become easily offended and vehemently defend those people and become very angry and resentful if you question their spending time with them. "It's okay. They're not using anymore." "Why don't you like them?" "They've changed." "I have no friends." "I need to have someone to hang out with." "I'm so bored. I'm going crazy." "I don't have anyone else." "I can handle it." "They won't do that around me."

- They withdraw and avoid you. They make excuses or say they're too busy.

We'd heard many times in recovery circles that if a person relapses and never stops using, then addiction has only three possible outcomes: jail, a mental institution, or death. I shuddered at the thought of any of them. It was staggering to think about. Appalling. *How can I let go of that?*

The next afternoon Reneé came home to collect her things. Before she left, we had the most adult, though sad, conversation we'd had with her up to that time. I can still see her in our small kitchen as she knelt down on the cool tile floor to pet Brie, the family dog. They had a special love for each other.

Reneé looked up at us with her big, green, bloodshot eyes, heavy makeup, and straggly black hair. She attempted to explain: "When I was in rehab, the old-timers in our support groups told us you know when you're done with drugs and drinking. I can't explain it, but I'm not done."

God, I can't believe this. Not after all she's been through and how far she's come. I don't think I can do this. Doesn't she realize there aren't any guarantees? Doesn't she know she might not get a second chance?

Reneé: On Relapse

When I came back from rehab to live with my parents, I was in bad shape, suffering severe PTSD from a violent mugging. It shook me to the core. I was also on some major painkillers, which I'm sure didn't help. Reckless with my sobriety, hanging out with friends who were using, inevitably I ended up using too. I remember being too trashed to come home, and so I called my dad to say I was going to stay the night with a friend. He asked if I had been using, and I couldn't lie. I told him the truth, and he told me I needed to come and get my things in the morning. My heart dropped to my stomach. I think I'd been hoping he wouldn't ask.

This was different from when I chose to leave home at eighteen. I didn't really want this, but I knew the rules. We'd had a clear conversation establishing that I could live at home with their full support as long as I was sober, and if I chose otherwise, they would refuse to enable me. I felt guilty and ashamed, but I wasn't mad at my parents.

Actually, when I told them I knew I wasn't done yet, knowing what it meant—as far as consequences from them—was a unique experience, because I stood in agreement with them: I had to leave. I felt a mixture

A WORD ABOUT ENABLING

Exactly what is enabling and how is it different from helping? Before we fell into the strange world of addiction, I didn't understand this at all. Our recovery groups taught us that enabling was reacting to people in a way that shields them from fully experiencing the harmful consequences of their behavior. Enabling differs from helping in that it allows people to be irresponsible. It's doing for others what they could and should be doing for themselves. Helping is doing something for someone who is incapable of doing it for himself.

of empowerment, fear, maturity, foolishness, courage, peace, and pain all at the same time.

On the one hand, it felt really beautiful to sit down and have such an honest conversation with them, even if it wasn't the ideal. The truth was being told, and it was a relief. I felt it was the right decision for me to leave. I didn't want to subject my family to anymore horror, especially when it came to my self-harm. I knew we would keep fighting, the tension would continue to disrupt their home, and it would affect my little sister. I couldn't bear the thought of carrying on that way any longer. I knew they'd keep trying to stop me and I would keep finding a way, and even in that dark space I wanted to respect my parents. Sneaking around felt almost worse to me than the destructive choices I was making. I've always valued authenticity and transparency. Even when I was doing something wrong, I wanted to be honest about it.

I can't emphasize enough how much I wanted to protect my mom and dad—not hurt them—and keep my sister from seeing me live that way. I knew she looked up to me, and I didn't want her to follow in my steps. I even got her in trouble a few times in my efforts to keep her away from some friends I thought would be a bad influence.

It's hard to see what we've been doing, to realize its potentially harmful effect on our child. It's extremely hard for us to change, to stop enabling, especially when it's a habit we've practiced for a long time. But if we don't at least try, we may be unintentionally aiding our loved ones in denying their problems. Our helpfulness can backfire and make it easier for our troubled child to stay sick longer. If we've played a part, it's better for their well-being that we stop, and the sooner the better. Why do we enable? It's complicated. For parents, Allison Bottke says it's for these reasons:

- we have confused "helping" with "enabling"
- we love too much, too little, too dependently, and too conditionally
- we fear for our children's safety, the consequences, and the unknown
- we feel guilty about things we did or didn't do when our children were younger
- we have never dealt with our own painful past issues, including abandonment, abuse, addictions, and a host of painful circumstances that shaped us into who we are
- our inborn personality traits make us more prone to do so
- it's all we know to do (habit)
- sometimes it's easier to maintain the status quo than it is to change
- we think it's the right thing to do as Christians
- we make excuses because drugs and alcohol have disabled or handicapped our adult children
- we are ignorant and don't know any better[16]

We need courage to ask ourselves some hard questions. It's important that we understand the deeper reasons behind what we're doing. The answers can be insightful for us in our own personal growth. Ask yourself,

- *What reward am I getting when I enable my child?*
- *In what ways does it make me feel better?*
- *What need is it filling in my own life?*
- *Can I see that my enabling might be harming my child at the same time it's benefitting me?*
- *Why do I repeatedly give second chances?*
- *What am I afraid of if I say no or refuse to help?*
- *Do I have the need to be in control? Why? To be liked? What's behind that?*

Talking with a friend or counselor would be advantageous. We need to get healthy ourselves. Taking a closer look at our underlying needs and motives can move us toward healthier relationships with everyone in our lives, not just our troubled kids.

Give yourself some grace if you've just realized you're an enabler. We try to take things into our own hands because we love our children so much. We're convinced they need our help. We want to protect them, fix them, solve their problems for them because we don't think they can do it on their own. We don't want them to hurt, to fail, to suffer any painful consequences. Forgive yourself now that you're aware this isn't a good thing to do like you thought it was.

After a lot of soul-searching and prayer, I came to better understand my reasons for enabling Reneé. When she was younger, I was her personal alarm clock. I drove her to school when she overslept and missed the bus. I made sure she passed her classes. I delivered her forgotten assignments or lunches. When she was older, I made excuses for unacceptable behavior. I ignored her disrespect too often. I gave second, third, and fourth chances. I believed her stories that sounded fishy. I was afraid to say no or refuse to help when she called and sounded needy. I gave money, paid medical bills, and provided a safety net when she had nowhere else to go. When I enabled in these ways, it felt loving. I thought I was being helpful. I've always liked to help.

I have a history of being a fixer too. Fixing problems made *me* feel better. I needed to feel in control of my daughter, especially when I thought she was in danger. I also needed to feel like I was doing something that could make a difference. *If I do this, then maybe she'll do that.* I thought it would guarantee acceptance and a certain improved outcome. It made me feel more secure in our relationship. I needed to protect her. It was too frightening not to step in and do something. I also needed to protect my reputation. *I'll look bad if I don't do this.*

But I discovered my enabling didn't really solve her problems at all. If anything, it might have made them worse had I continued.

BOUNDARIES

I've learned that we parents need to work on being healthy ourselves. We need clear, strong boundaries for us as well as for our kids. We each have to determine *I'll go this far and no further.* When you help, do you find that you feel angry later on? Your anger is a good barometer. Do you feel resentful? That feeling is telling you something's wrong. Do you feel let down or cynical? Nervous? Irritable? Anxious? You probably crossed a boundary you didn't realize you needed. Boundaries help you disengage with your emotions and keep your sanity. They help you determine what's your responsibility and what's not, what you're comfortable with and what you're not. Boundaries keep you from being exploited physically, emotionally, or financially. They empower you to say no.

We set external boundaries for our kids while they're growing up (think of them as rules): "No playing in the street." "Don't push your sister down." "Be home by dark." "Don't talk back to me." When they become teenagers, a boundary might be that they can't smoke pot in your home or skip school. If they do, there will be a consequence, and it must be enforced consistently.

A boundary you might have for yourself would be that if your child steals from you, you'll report them to the police. Another one might be that you expect to be treated respectfully—no cussing or slamming doors in your face. Or they're responsible to pay for any speeding tickets they may get. When you model having healthy boundaries, it's good for your child's emotional maturity. For them the goal is to develop their own internal boundaries by the time they're on their own. For you, it's to not let your child run the show, not lose your temper and do or say something you'll regret, so you won't develop negative attitudes toward them. Read books about boundaries.[17] And consulting a counselor would be wise. You've heard that over and over again, haven't you?

When we no longer need to enable or feel rewarded for doing so, we'll find the strength to say, "No, I'm sorry, but I've decided I can't [or won't] help you with that anymore. But I'm confident you'll solve this problem on your own. I believe you can do it!"

When Reneé was still legally a minor, a few of our boundaries were that she had a curfew as well as restrictions on where she could go with friends (no nightclubs or concerts where they served alcohol and not at anyone's home if their parents weren't there), no watching R-rated or X-rated movies, no listening to heavy metal or death metal music, and no guys staying overnight. When she turned eighteen and had a substance abuse problem, she could live with us only if she was actively working on her recovery. She couldn't smoke in our home, and she was responsible for paying her own bills. We told her not to call us if she was arrested and needed to be bailed out, because the answer would be no. We agreed to pay for rehab once, period. After that it would be her responsibility. And as a result of receiving many traumatic middle-of-the-night phone calls, I began to set my phone on vibrate when I went to bed. I put it far away from where I slept so I couldn't hear anything. This was essential for my own sanity.

Brené Brown says boundaries are establishing for me "what's okay and what's not okay."[18] It's not easy to set boundaries and follow through. It's a lot of hard work, but it's the most loving thing we can do for ourselves. We can grow strong enough to do this. If I did, I bet you can too.

When we erect boundaries, our kids may fail. If they do, their pain will hurt us more than they can imagine. They may accuse, "You don't care." Even though it feels like it's killing you, you need to ignore them. They can't understand now. One day maybe they will. It reminds me of when you took your child to preschool or the church nursery the first time. They cried, screamed, and threw a fit. All you, the parent, wanted to do was to rescue them from their discomfort. The teacher told you, "He'll be fine. This is normal. They all feel this way. But give it some time. They'll adjust and be okay. You'll see how they thrive. You're doing a good job, Mom. Keep up the good work. Be strong."

If we let our children struggle and fail, they'll learn more than if we come to their rescue. We need to quit trying to control what we can't control. Trying to only makes things worse. When we stop interfering, it might even motivate them to want to change sooner. Some pain now could spare them years of pain later.

Yes, our children will struggle, but we must choose to step back. We need to give them the opportunity to prove to themselves that they can solve problems—or not—on their own. They may experience hard consequences such as jail time because we refused to bail them out or have to pay a fine or be evicted from an apartment because of past-due bills or end up in the psych ward because they quit taking their meds. As a result, they'll reach their lowest point sooner and hopefully decide they're ready to deal with their addiction or other challenging issues, learn painful lessons, get the chance to grow from them, and hopefully develop self-confidence. We don't want to rob them of those things, do we?

A dad shared with me about when he and his wife finally found the courage to tell their son he had to find somewhere else to live unless he was ready to stop abusing substances and consent to go into rehab immediately. At first their son was angry, but then he came to his senses. He agreed he had a problem and went into a treatment program a few days later. It changed his life. "It was one of the hardest, most frightening things we ever did, but one of the best," this dad commented.

Reneé: On Boundaries

I didn't ever hate my parents for telling me I had to move out. My motivation was inner pain that I didn't know how to deal with. I was absolutely hurt, but I think most of the hurt was more for my parents, for the pain I was causing them. I think my lack of anger was also an indicator of my lack of self-love. I didn't care enough about myself to want to fight for a home, to prove that I was right or they were wrong. I didn't care what happened to me. I was in too much pain. I was too busy trying to run away and numb my trauma to feel angry at someone who clearly loved me and wasn't to blame.

They didn't blindside me. I had been given fair warning, and I made my choice. Many people have a hard time understanding why I wasn't angry or resentful. Morally and logically I understood why these boundaries where set in place. The sick parts of me were grateful to be out of the house, where I was able to feed my addiction without any obstacles, house rules, or sneaking around.

I had friends whose parents kicked them out who felt the complete opposite of me. They fought to stay, begged and pleaded, and had such hatred for their parents. Some of them were blindsided; they came home one day to find their things on the lawn and the locks changed. That might have made me really angry too. I also know that a lot of these kids cleaned up pretty quickly or got help because they weren't willing to live on the streets or go from couch to couch. It was effective.

A lot of the anger your child might feel is also a mixture of fear. I know it was the case for a lot of my friends who had to move out. They had no idea how they would survive without the help of their family (car, money, food, and so on), and the idea of being homeless was terrifying. Where I was different was that I'd become so detached

(continued on the next page)

and reckless that I didn't care where I ended up. I don't think I entirely cared if I survived, either.

Today, nearly everyone I've met in recovery has a deep sense of gratitude and respect for the boundaries their parents set when they were sick. Those boundaries allowed them to hit rock bottom a lot faster and, therefore, pursue recovery much sooner. The anger they had at the time has been replaced with love. Now they have strong, healthy relationships with their families.

It really upsets me when I see parents and lovers of people suffering with addictions who are too afraid to set firm boundaries and stick to them. Sadly, many end up dying because they never experienced the full consequences of their addiction; it just kept being cushioned and swept under the rug. Their loved ones never stopped helping them. They thought it was unloving to say no. They thought their children would resent them, that other people would think they were bad parents, or that they had failed, so they enabled.

Without pain there's no motivation to change anything.

I encourage you—I implore you—to set firm, healthy boundaries and don't waver from them. Refuse to enable your child's addiction.

Boundaries do not mean you're turning your love off or giving up. Boundaries mean you refuse to believe your child can't change. By saying no, you give them permission to say yes to love themselves, to live as the beautiful, present, empowered person they can be. Be intentional by reminding them you love them, that you'll be there for them the moment they're willing to choose a healthy lifestyle, that you'll help them when they want it. If you're met with anger from your child when you enforce a boundary, don't own it. Remember, you're dealing with a disease, and that disease is what's angry at you. The devil's also angry at you for not helping him destroy your kid. This is not the person your child really is. Remember the story of Jekyll and Hyde?

Hold on to the truth that you're not doing this to punish or harm or be vindictive. You're doing the best you can to help, to love, and to fight for them, knowing that ultimately they have to choose to fight for themselves.

And hold on to hope, allowing God's peace to comfort you. The truth is that they are His creation, His children, and He's with them every moment. There's no guarantee, but you can say that you did your best. It's far better to know you did all you could than to look back later and say you wish you wouldn't have been too afraid to do what would really help them.

The hardest things we choose out of love give the deepest, most profound gifts to our souls. So don't be afraid to have and keep your boundaries. By far one of the most loving things my parents did was to set clear, strong boundaries with me. They told me if I chose destructive behaviors (to drink or use drugs), they would not be a part of it, and I couldn't live with them. They refused to stand by and help me destroy myself. They assured me that they loved me very much and that nothing would ever change that. They also told me if and when I was ready to get clean, they would do anything they could to help, and I would have their full support. I could count on them to be there for me. There's nothing hateful about that.

The minute I made a choice for love and life, my parents were there to support me just as they promised. They kept their word. They were a powerful, beautiful representation of God's love, which is unchanging: "If you choose to go away, I won't keep you here. But if you choose Me, I'm here 100 percent whenever you're ready."

I respected my mom and dad for that. I never spoke badly about them for what they did. I understood. I strongly believe that my parents' choice to love me enough to let me go was a key part in my process. If I had been allowed to go on living with them, I would've been robbed of fully experiencing the consequences of my actions, and I'm sure I wouldn't have asked for help as soon as I did.

Another couple, after having their drug-addicted daughter steal and pawn their possessions (jewelry, computers, and so on) countless times, denying she had a problem, finally drew the line and had her arrested for the thefts. They gave her an ultimatum. Get help for her addiction, or move out and they would stop supporting her financially. She experienced some hard consequences: being arrested, going to jail, fines, probation, mandatory counseling and treatment. At last she decided she was ready to get help. Today, she's in recovery, has a part-time job, is in college, has her own apartment, and has a healthy relationship with her parents. Her mom said, "I never thought I could turn in my own daughter, but I was becoming so bitter and angry. It was the last thing I wanted to do, but I finally realized, by protecting her and making excuses, I wasn't really helping her. Our enabling had to stop. It turned out to be exactly what she needed."

Remind yourself of this the next time you're tempted to offer assistance when it would be better not to. It means trusting God even more than you already have. We'll have many chances to exercise our trust muscles during the journey. As we do, we'll grow stronger and stronger along the way.

But don't be too hard on yourself if you fall back into enabling habits from time to time. Remember, you're not perfect. Easy does it, Al-Anon urges. It's not easy to quit enabling, but we need to, because it's the right thing to do for us *and* for our kids. When you feel your resolve weakening, it can help to talk to someone who will encourage you to be strong, such as another parent who understands, a counselor, or a support group.

By no longer enabling, we can help our children become mature, independent adults. We can help them reach rock bottom so they're ready to change their harmful behaviors. We allow them to learn how to fly (or not) on their own. We can begin to live our own lives and let them live theirs. Our children then suffer the consequences for their poor choices, but we don't.

LIVING THROUGH RELAPSE

I'll never forget how Tom remained calm and composed when Reneé told him she wasn't finished with drugs and alcohol, although I knew he was dying inside. "Reneé, honey, you don't get to choose what 'done' might mean. It could mean you end up in jail, a mental institution, or worse—dead." His words gave me chills.

Regretfully, with a tear in her eye, she said, "I know, Dad, I know. I'm so sorry."

There was no anger. No yelling. No angst. Just an honest admission on her part and the heavy burden of an unknown outcome on ours. She ran back upstairs to get a few more things, taking two at a time the way she used to. A few minutes later she dragged two large trash bags down the stairs stuffed with her belongings. *I wonder if her favorite razor blade is in there.*

Maintaining my composure was a monumental task. Everything in me wanted to grab her by the arms and force her to stay, make her listen, make her do the right thing. The three of us hugged and kissed in the middle of the living room as the afternoon sun peeked through the blinds. We took turns saying "I love you," and then she was gone—again.

That was one of my lowest points. Her departure was very loving and peaceful yet intensely heartbreaking. It felt like a death blow. *Good-bye, Reneé, I hope to see you again someday, but not in the morgue. God, I hate being so powerless. Can You really redeem this? Help me trust You more.*

Not knowing where my daughter was and not hearing from her for weeks at a time felt like torture, like a living nightmare. A friend in recovery gently reminded us of the hard realities: "I hate to say this, but when you can't find an addict, they're either on a binge or they're dead." His words made me cringe. They seemed cruel, yet I knew he was trying to prepare us. *Dear God, please don't let Reneé die.*

The frequency and terror of my nightmares increased. The dark cloud of depression returned. Crying most of the time, I chose to isolate again. I didn't want anyone to know what was happening or ask me about my daughter. The only good thing was, when she left, the angst left with her. Only now I had to cope with the strain of not knowing where she was or what was happening to her.

You may ask, if I had healthy boundaries and had enforced them, then why was I just as miserable as before? I didn't know this then, but here's the key to using boundaries to get more stability and contentment: being able to detach. It's not enough to lay down the law and mean it; you have to let your child go and surrender them into God's care. You have to let go of the illusion of control. And then you begin to heal, whether they do or not.

I didn't understand that relapse is often part of recovery. Some addicts go through rehab four, five, six times (or more) before they truly get sober and are ready to begin new lives. Some time ago I met a man who told me it took him nine stints in rehab to really grasp sobriety. *Nine!* When I met him he was the director of a rehab program. His testimony encouraged me to lower my expectations and focus on taking care of myself instead of stressing about my daughter. He helped me realize that relapse didn't mean permanent failure. She was still alive, so her fall wasn't final.

Did you hear that? If your child is still alive, then their fall isn't final. It's not over yet.

For us it just meant she would have to pick herself up and begin again. I needed to be strong enough to let go of what I was powerless over. Then I could move forward. I needed to learn this new skill—to detach. It would help make peace with having no control.

How do you respond to having no control? Do you become manipulative and demanding? Do you get angry and loud? Do you dig in your heels and try harder? Do you become depressed and fall into despair?

Hear this: it's not your fault—unless you encouraged your child's behavior and aided in their destruction. You cannot control this. Stop trying and quit blaming yourself or anyone else.

The only person we can control is ourself. There's nothing we can do to make our children want to change or speed up the healing process. But don't forget, God is still in control. He has sovereign authority over the final outcome of their lives and of ours. With a world full of sinful, rebellious people, He gave them the freedom to choose, but it doesn't mean He makes them do what He wants. Yes, He's been in control of the course of human history and of the whole world since time began. Even though it doesn't always look like it, He's there, always working behind the scenes. Watching. Waiting. Wooing.

Remember that. Reprogram your self-talk. Print *God is in control* on a sticky note and look at it a hundred times a day if necessary. Other healthy self-talk would be:

- *I'm not alone.*
- *God loves me.*
- *God is with me.*
- *With His help, I'm going to get through this.*
- *I'm going to be okay.*
- *Whatever happens, God loves my child more than I do, and He's with them.*
- *God cares about my pain.*
- *I will survive this.*
- *Don't look too far ahead, stay in the present moment.*

Al-Anon sayings are great too: *I can't control it. I can't change it. I can't cure it. One day at a time. Let go and let God.*

And remember this too: "Is anything too hard for the LORD?" (Genesis 18:14). My head said *no,* but to be honest, my heart said *maybe.* It's easy to know something intellectually but harder to really believe it in your heart. It's a pretty normal reaction for the parents of troubled kids.

LEARNING TO DETACH

Tom and I first learned about detachment at a conference for parents of addicts. I wasn't sure I had the strength or courage to let go of Reneé. I was too nice, too scared, and too weak. Besides, it felt cruel, unloving. I've talked to many hurting parents who have the same opinion. Confused, they don't believe detaching is the right thing to do. In our culture, to detach often means being indifferent, disinterested, unconcerned, not caring. Perhaps that's why it feels confusing and wrong. But this isn't what they promote in recovery circles.

The kind of detaching they recommend is to separate ourselves from the adverse effects of another person's destructive behaviors. Physical separation isn't always required. It's neither kind nor unkind. It doesn't imply judgment or condemnation. It's not cutting ourselves off from the people we care about but from the agony of our involvement with them. Detachment helps us to be more objective.

Our recovery groups taught us there's nothing we can say or do to cause *or* to stop another person's destructive behavior. We're not responsible for our children's problems or their recovery from them. Detaching allows us to let go of our obsession with them. Then we can begin to lead happier, healthier lives. We can live with dignity. We can still love them without liking their behavior. When we begin to stop enabling, we begin to detach. We start reaping emotional and psychological rewards. Through detachment we can learn to stop

- suffering because of the actions or reactions of other people
- allowing ourselves to be used or abused by others in the interest of their own needs
- doing for others what they can do for themselves
- manipulating situations so others will eat, go to bed, get up, pay bills, not drink or use drugs, or behave the way we want them to

- covering up for someone else's mistakes or misdeeds
- preventing a crisis if one will occur in the natural course of events

I knew I was learning to detach when I stopped looking at Reneé's social media pages, stopped calling to check up on her, slept better without the torment of wondering if she was safe, quit calling her friends to ask if they'd seen her or what they thought about her condition, worried

Reneé: On Relapse and Detaching

It's said that relapse is a part of recovery, and I believe it's true. It isn't a requirement, but it's often a part of the process. Relapse, to me, is synonymous with the human condition, which is to be fallible. That word *relapse* used to terrify me. The idea of screwing up, losing everything I'd worked so hard for, starting over, and all of the what-ifs used to keep me up at night. I don't see it that way anymore. I've learned that at the foundation of everything is either fear or love—and we always have a choice. Fear-based anxiety and guessing about the future are not from God. They don't serve anyone.

If you're worried about your child's recovery, detach. Let them go. You can't predict the future. Recognize the lies that are causing you pain, validate those feelings, and speak them. Ask God what He wants to say to you about your fears and own what He reveals to you.

Only the truth will give you peace. If things are going well with your child's recovery, allow yourself to experience that gift. You can't control their process or the future. You can only do your part. The best thing you can do is to love and accept your child (and yourself) through this journey. I encourage you to detach in a healthy way yet remain loving, authentic, and steadfast, regardless of what your child is choosing.

less about the consequences she might face, didn't feel guilty about not helping financially or not paying her medical bills, no longer reminded her about taking care of important details and didn't feel bad about it, and when I could put her problems out of my mind. I knew I was making progress because I was gradually experiencing more peace and less angst. I could focus more on myself and my life and less on hers.

The process of detaching is hard for everyone in the family. Human nature typically associates significant change with stress. We're going to feel the strain, but it's okay because of what it can produce. And it can be just as difficult for us to change our patterns as it is for our teen-to-adult kids to change theirs. Old habits die hard, no matter your age.

When we learn to detach, we stop denying our own feelings and needs. Focusing on ourselves and allowing our children to experience the consequences of their actions will improve our sense of well-being. We can let go of the false belief that our children have to be okay before we can be okay. Tom and I still cared deeply. We still had concerns and felt sad for Reneé, but it no longer overwhelmed us. We were taking back our lives, and it felt great.

Dear hurting parent, the hardest practice for me was learning to let go. When I say to let go, I mean that we allow God to hold our children. They belong to Him and He's with them (and you) always. Reneé says, when we let go, we can love without an agenda. We can hope without expectation.

GUARDING THE FAMILY

During stressful times, Tom and I found ourselves at odds with each other more and more. Overwhelmed with a sense of powerlessness, we took turns feeling angry or sad. Any stress puts a marriage at risk, especially this kind. No one is immune. Relentless pressure builds up over time and takes a toll. We say things we don't mean. We hurt each other easily. We build walls. We push each other away because we don't understand one another. Sometimes we take our anger out on our mate because it feels too risky to vent on our child if they're in a fragile state.

When it feels like our world's falling apart, we need to mutually support one another, make our spouse feel safe, and wrap our arms around each other. We're in this battle together. It's essential we go through it on the same page and present a united front. If we don't take the necessary steps to protect our marriage, it can become another victim of our child's issues. Tom and I didn't want to let that happen to ours. We had a choice. We didn't have to be powerless about this. We could do something. So can you.

A couple we knew who were going through a similar challenge came to the same conclusion.

The wife shared with me, "As our son rebelled and made poor choices, tension grew in our home. Confusion over what to do and fear of what could happen resulted in a hurting marriage. I'm grateful that one day my husband made a choice that he would do whatever it took to protect us, to align our hearts, and to stand firm as one. Our son is still on a difficult journey, but our marriage remains strong." *I want that too, Lord.*

We decided to guard our marriage by being more intentional about our relationship. We made sure that after the Lord we put each other first, then our children came next. It's so easy for kids, especially troubled ones, to slip into first or second place. Before we know it, they've become like idols and our marriages have moved to last place. Our beloved sons and daughters subtly and gradually become too important. We give them too much of our attention and energy. We're not bad for doing this. We've just got things out of order.

After they're out on their own, living healthily or unhealthily as they choose, we'll have just each other, as we did in the beginning. If we aren't careful, what will be left of us then? Tom and I determined to be proactive by doing the following:

- We prayed together regularly.
- We went to church every week, even when we didn't feel

like it. Worship was a balm, and the message was often exactly what we needed.

- We joined a small group and honestly shared our pain.
- We planned weekly date nights and declared them "no-prodigal zones" (no talking about Reneé was allowed). Difficult to do, but very good for us.
- We allowed for some controlled venting when necessary. Sometimes on our way to a restaurant, one of us would say, "I need five minutes to get some things off my chest. Is that okay?" We'd agree, then make ourselves stop when the time was up.
- We gave each other permission to feel our feelings and to not always feel the same way. Our emotions would flip-flop. One would feel angry and callous while the other felt empathetic and overly sensitive. Then we'd switch. We decided we'd just roll with whatever we were feeling and not try to change or fix each other.
- We were quick to forgive.
- We learned to listen better.
- Once a year we tried to attend a marriage conference or retreat to focus on improving our relationship.

When Reneé was in rehab, we always participated in the program's family weekends and therapy groups. They were very beneficial. You may also want to seek out a good marriage counselor. Contact the churches in your area to see which offers counseling centers. You can also find local therapists at www.therapists.psychologytoday.com. You can even refine your search for Christian counselors.

We also realized we needed to guard our relationships with our other children. We still needed to think about Michael and April. It's easy to give troubled sons or daughters all the attention. They're very needy, but that means their siblings may get neglected. Resentment can grow, which ends up causing more problems. Their troubled brother or sister took you away. Because of the problem child, the others got less of you, the left-overs. It really isn't fair.

You never want that to happen. You love them as much as the prodigal. They're no less worthy of your time and attention. The following analogy helped Michael and April to understand. We explained that when one part of our physical body is injured or diseased, it requires extra focus and attention. But it's temporary, for a season. It doesn't mean the other parts are loved or valued any less. They're just as important, but their sister needed more from us for a while. This made sense to them.

These things can also help mend the relationship with your other kids:

- Lavish positive attention on them.
- Plan special outings to do what they enjoy. We planned a special fly-fishing trip to Colorado for April and the two of us. Lessons from a professional were a real treat.
- Compliment them often for their strengths and accomplishments. Tell them frequently how much you appreciate them and their good behavior.
- Do your best to attend every activity and special event. We made sure we never missed a soccer game.
- Reward them for making good choices. We encouraged April to have friends over often and planned special outings.
- Be sure they're informed about what's happening with their brother or sister in age-appropriate ways (we kept it from April when she was younger). It means a lot to them to know what's going on. April was always included in family visits when Reneé was in rehab. Her brother lived in another city, so he wasn't as involved, but he was always supportive of her and visited when he could.

Be extra careful not to react to your other children in the same way you would their troubled sibling. To protect your other children emotionally, spiritually, and physically from a dangerous sibling (which Reneé never was), do all you can to give them separate rooms. You may need to allow them to put an extra lock on their door (you can keep the key if they want). Be alert for trouble, and always be quick to defend them.

Don't overlook unacceptable behavior or let the harassing sibling get away with mistreating their brothers or sisters. It's easier to let it go, because it takes a lot of emotional effort when you're already running low on that commodity, but it's absolutely necessary. Your other children need to feel safe and supported. If they've already suffered, it would be wise to give them some time with a counselor to talk things through. You may even want to look for a way to give them a respite from the chaos. Is there a relative they could go visit over the summer, over a weekend, or even for a night? They probably need a break too, like you do.

Another thing to watch out for is that sometimes, if we see even the slightest hint of concerning behavior similar to our troubled child, we're quick to become fearful and jump to unfair conclusions about our other children. April had to remind us of this on a number of occasions. "Mom, Dad, I'm *not* Reneé." What a good wake-up call. She was right. We had to ask her to forgive us several times.

THE POWER OF POWERLESSNESS

Aware of having no control, we knew that any day we could receive a phone call telling us what we never wanted to hear. We needed help to survive but didn't know where to turn. Slowly, we began to reach out, and when we did, little by little, we found help. Our own healing gradually came.

Why do we seek help as a last resort? For us, it was difficult to surrender to the idea that we, who were usually competent, didn't have a clue about handling our situation. We didn't want to admit we'd failed as parents (we hadn't, but that's how we felt) or didn't have our act together. We'd been dealt a hand of cards we had no idea how to play. Should we turn and run or just fake it? Our natural impulse was to fake it and try to take control. This only caused more trouble. We finally realized we had to yield all our concerns for our girl into the hands of her Maker. When we truly accepted our inability and powerlessness over Reneé, we stopped trying to force her to do what we wanted her to do. Another recovery phrase that came to mean a lot to us says, "I can't. God can. I think I'll let Him."

Admitting we were powerless wasn't a statement of despair. On the contrary, it helped us accept our limitations and lean hard on the Lord. We knew we couldn't make it without Him. On our own we'd fizzle out. This acceptance prepared us to face what we couldn't cope with using the resources we had, which weren't enough. Acceptance produced the ability to do what Reneé talked about in her comments, the hardest thing of all: to let go.

What does it really mean to let go? I like what Charles R. Swindoll highlighted in *The Grace Awakening:*

To let go does not mean to stop caring,
> it means I can't do it for someone else.

To let go is not to cut myself off,
> it's the realization that I can't control another

To let go is not to enable,
> but to allow learning from natural consequences.

To let go is to admit powerlessness,
> which means the outcome is not in my hands.

To let go is not to try to change or blame another,
> I can only change myself.

To let go is not to care for,
> but to care about.

To let go is not to fix,
> but to be supportive.

To let go is not to judge,
> but to allow another to be a human being.

To let go is not to be in the middle arranging all the outcomes,
> but to allow others to effect their own outcomes.

To let go is not to be protective;
    it is to permit another to face reality.
To let go is not to deny,
    but to accept.
To let go is not to nag, scold, or argue,
    but to search out my own shortcomings and to correct them.
To let go is not to adjust everything to my desires,
    but to take each day as it comes.
To let go is not to criticize and regulate anyone,
    but to try to become what dream I can be.
To let go is not to regret the past,
    but to grow and to live for the future.
To let go is to fear less and love more![19]

The pain of seeing our children destroy themselves feels unbearable. How can we let go and detach? These are our dearly loved children. We'd gladly give our lives for them. When you come to the place where you need to relinquish your child to the Lord, you may be helped by using the following two prayers. They've been empowering for me by helping me to release Reneé back to God. I encourage you to write them on a sheet of paper or print them out, personalize them, and keep them handy.

Lord, [child's name] is yours. Her/his life is in Your hands. I release her/him into Your care. As much as I love [child's name], You love her/him more. I give [child's name] back to You. Please do something, and hurry.
    In Your mighty name.
    Amen.

"Hear my cry, O God; listen to my prayer. From the ends of the earth I call to you on behalf of [child's name], I call as my heart grows faint; lead me to the rock that is higher than I" [see Psalm

61:1–2]. Father, do whatever it takes to rescue [child's name]. Make her/him uncomfortable with her/his condition. Cause her/him to long for relief. Show [child's name] how futile life is without You. Convince her/him that she/he can come to You; You never turn anyone away. When she/he cries out to you, come quickly, precious Savior, come quickly!

By faith, I thank You for what You're doing in [child's name] right now.

In Jesus's name.

Amen.

Even though we may feel lost and powerless, like Alice in Wonderland, when we cry out to God, He'll help us to stop enabling and detach in love so we can let go of our troubled kids. And remember, we don't release our precious children into nothingness, but rather into the hands of their Creator, the lover of their souls. What could be better than that?

Scripture That Helps

We were under great pressure, far beyond our ability to endure, so that we despaired of life itself. Indeed, we felt we had received the sentence of death. But this happened that we might not rely on ourselves but on God, who raises the dead. (2 Corinthians 1:8–9)

[We pray] that God will grant them repentance leading them to a knowledge of the truth, and that they will come to their senses and escape from the trap of the devil, who has taken them captive to do his will. (2 Timothy 2:25–26)

10

Exhaustion: What's the Remedy?

Life is a walk. Each day we take steps. Our tomorrow is determined by the steps we take today.

—Stormie Omartian, *Just Enough Light for the Step I'm On*

Are you on the verge of collapse? Burned out from the constant stress and strain from the unexpected challenges you've had to deal with? We've all experienced exhaustion before. The feeling of being depleted of emotional and physical energy, fatigued on every level, with no reserves left to draw on. You've scraped the bottom of your emotional barrel and come up empty-handed. When I reached this point, too weary to handle any more crises very well, I felt on the verge of collapse. Sometimes parenting can bring us to the point of total burnout. We feel completely inadequate. *Oh no, I don't have what I need for the job.* Emotional exhaustion takes a toll.

When Reneé's issues loomed, I felt as though I dragged through the day, barely putting one foot in front of the other. Completely defeated.

If you've been on this journey for a prolonged period of time, you may feel you're holding on by a thread. There's something you need if you're going to make it to the end and thrive again: resilience.

What is resilience and what does it look like? How can we develop it?

Do you think you're a resilient person? Why do brokenhearted parents need it?

Sometimes I find it easier to understand what something is when I first understand what it's not. To be resilient is not being defeated, rigid, or inflexible. It's not letting adversity shape you. It's not giving up. It's refusing to let stress knock you down.

Has your parenting experience made you hardhearted, indifferent, or calloused? Overcome and overwhelmed, have you given up or wanted to? If so, then you need to pack some resilience in your life's travel bag.

Let's look at what resilience is. *Resilient people are able to recover quickly from adversity, changes, or setbacks.* They adapt well to challenges and serious losses. They bounce back from trials and troubles. They're strong and flexible under extreme pressure. If you're resilient, when you fall off the proverbial horse, you hop right back on. When I was twenty, I fell off a horse—a real one. I thought I broke my hip. After hobbling around for a week in awful pain, I vowed I'd never get on another one. Thirty years went by before I did. I wasn't very tough back then.

I needed resilience, that hard-to-describe character trait that permits a person to experience extreme hardships, get knocked down, yet not stay down long. Instead, they're able to rebound with increased strength and vigor. "They find a way to rise from the ashes."[20]

In what ways have you felt stretched out of shape from being your child's parent? Your story might be a lot like mine. My experiences were life altering, traumatizing, and bone wearying. My zest for life vanished. The heart-wrenching situations in our children's lives can do this to us. Our kids can push us beyond our breaking point until we finally pop. Emotionally, mentally, and spiritually deflated, we may even lose our will to live.

GET STRETCHIER

Can you think of some resilient things? Rubber bands, trampolines, elastic waistbands, headbands, ponytail holders, wristbands, exercise or tension balls, bungee cords, skin (especially during pregnancy), balloons, and Silly Putty (remember that?). In the Disney movie *The Incredibles,* one animated character, Elastigirl, had the unique ability to stretch her body like a super-duper bungee cord. Her elasticity made it possible to do things that would ordinarily have been impossible.

Take a minute now to find something flexible or stretchy, like a rubber band. As you read the rest of this chapter, pull on it as a visual aid while you think about becoming resilient.

What happens when you blow up a balloon beyond its capacity? It bursts. Your emotions are like that. If you stretch them too far, you'll burst too. *Fiddler on the Roof* has a powerful scene in which the youngest daughter, who has married outside the family's faith, comes to her father and pleads for his blessing. But as much as he loves her, it's too much. He can't. He doesn't have the emotional capacity to adapt. His response is, "If I bend that far I'll break!"

What's your breaking point? Have you already experienced it? If so, remember how you handled the crisis. Were you stretchy? Did you adapt and bounce back or did you break, becoming angry, hardened, and defeated?

As parents with broken hearts, we need resilience to help us persevere and endure instead of collapsing. In other words, emotionally, we need to be like a bouncy ball or a piece of elastic—able to stretch but not break. That's a mental image I hope you can visualize. Imagine yourself snapping back. Is it possible?

I know, you may not be able to do all this adapting and overcoming yet. In the early years of my parenting journey, I couldn't. I was too broken. Some days were unbearable. Survival meant digging deep to find a way for this painful trial not to destroy me, not only for my sake but for the sake of my dear husband and other two children. There were still people who loved me and needed me. They mattered too. What about them? They deserved to have me fully present in their lives. Reneé's welfare couldn't be the center of my world, although I'd allowed it to be. I still had a life of my own to live—if I could.

Are we born resilient? Opinions vary, but I think it can be developed. Some people tend naturally toward resilience. If that's not you, don't be discouraged. I'm convinced the potential lies in all of us. If you lacked this toughness of spirit in the past, things can be different in the future.

BECOMING RESILIENT

Here are eight ways I grew some resilience in my soul.

1. I Simplified My Life

Someone suggested this and it sounded strange but good. Simplifying meant cutting back, saying no to every extra, nonessential activity for a season until strength returned. I was involved in a number of activities, and it was hard to step away from them. I found it best to make calls and send e-mails without lengthy explanations: "I'm sorry, but I'm not able to participate in this right now. It's not permanent, but I don't know when I'll be able to help again. I'll let you know if I can in the future. Thank you for understanding."

Most were very understanding, but that didn't matter. I knew it was what I had to do. It created margin in my life. Breathing room. Space. How wonderful to be freed up, to have time for rest when it was really needed. Simplifying helped lower stress and preserve emotional energy, which was wonderful. I needed the little I had in order to survive.

2. I Developed a Community of Authentic Relationships

Yes, I've said it before, but it's worth repeating because it's so hard to do: find like-minded people who can encourage you and whom you can encourage. On my recovery journey I needed places where I could be real and accepted. I had plenty to process. Guilt and shame had prompted my husband and me to hide and isolate. Both of us were bundles of nerves, so we finally swallowed our pride and trudged into an Al-Anon meeting. We knew we needed to be with people who'd walked in our shoes.

To our surprise, we felt safe and understood, able to share our inner struggles. Our refusal to continue withdrawing facilitated our finding others to journey with. Step by step, seeing authenticity modeled, we opened up. Everyone was real. No one was shocked. The degree of caring and acceptance felt like that of church—a sacred, safe place.

Support groups like Al-Anon turned out to be one of the healthiest things I participated in to become resilient because they helped me process my feelings in the context of community instead of trying to cope alone. We really do need each other more than we know.

3. I Enlisted Steady Spiritual Support

Tom and I felt better going to the meetings, but something was missing. The support groups we'd joined couldn't offer the depth of spiritual input we needed: a focus on the Word of God, spiritual truth, and prayer. These things were foundational for our hope and strength. That's the reason we decided to start our own support group a few years later when we felt ready. To prepare, we gleaned the best elements from Al-Anon and several other groups we'd been part of. Seven years later we're still leading groups. We also help others start them all over the country, and we love it. We're convinced support groups are a critical lifesaver for hurting parents.

Fellowship with my church family, my small group, and Bible study groups was crucial. Welcoming a sponsor and counselors into my life helped too. God met me, ministered to me, and strengthened me through His people. Not in isolation, but in the body of Christ, the church. I could share my struggles with openness and authenticity. I could receive supernatural help. I could be loved, listened to, prayed for, and upheld in amazing ways.

We can't get through this difficult experience in a good way on our own. If we think we can, we're fooling ourselves. The worst thing we can do is stay alone. Seclusion weakens us, but connecting with other heart-broken parents strengthens us. Building a reliable support system of strong friendships with trustworthy, caring, nonjudgmental people is an incredible resource. Permitting them on my journey has made it possible for God to minister to me through them. How much I would have missed had I not opened my heart to them.

4. I Nurtured My Personal Faith in God

In the beginning my faith was shaken. I questioned what I believed about suffering, parenting, prayer, and God's goodness. Somehow I found the strength to keep picking up my Bible almost every day. There were times I didn't, feeling too dead inside, unable to concentrate, but thankfully those occasions were rare. Usually I forced myself to read His Word no matter how I felt. Some days a paragraph or one sentence was all I could manage. But I kept at it, certain of my need for the spiritual sustenance it could provide. I believed it was the main way my heavenly Father would refresh my exhausted soul.

Strengthening my faith included cultivating a strong prayer life. I poured out my heart, freely expressing my feelings. Sometimes prayer was a lament: complaining and mourning and grieving. Sometimes my prayer was full of questioning, venting anger and frustration. Other times I mostly listened for His still, small voice. Extended time alone with my Good Shepherd became like healing oil for my wounded spirit. After a while, I scheduled a half-day every month at a park or other peaceful place, away from distractions. In a relaxed setting I read, rested, prayed, walked, and journaled. I'd sit in the warm sunshine or under the shade of a tree and look at a lake, the sky, a large cross in a garden, and occasionally sing a favorite hymn or praise chorus. That's where I started to write this book. I always returned home renewed.

Developing resilience requires a lot of trust in God: "Those who hope in the LORD will renew their strength. They will soar on wings like

eagles; they will run and not grow weary, they will walk and not be faint"
(Isaiah 40:31). This verse describes endurance, persisting in the face of
trials, bouncing back from the verge of collapse. By drawing closer to our
Good Shepherd, tapping into His strength, we can discover the ability to
endure. We can overcome exhaustion: "For though the righteous fall
seven times, they rise again" (Proverbs 24:16). He's the One who will
enable us to adapt and spring back stronger. When we're stretched and
pulled beyond our limits, He won't let us break, even though it may not
feel that way. By choosing to stay close to Him, strengthening and nurturing our faith, we can handle any crisis.

H. Norman Wright observed,

> Resilient people have a creed that says, "I believe!" and they
> affirm their creed daily. In essence they say:
> - I believe God's promises are true.
> - I believe heaven is real.
> - I believe God will see me through.
> - I believe nothing can separate us from God's love.
> - I believe God has work for me to do.[21]

5. I Improved My Physical Health

I started a health plan that included eating better, drinking plenty of
water, getting adequate rest, and giving attention to other medical needs.
I made appointments with doctors, counselors, or clergy as needed. I ex-
ercised regularly, which released endorphins and naturally improved a
sense of well-being. Even a fifteen-minute walk was rejuvenating. This
also helped me process my grief. In short, I gave myself permission to
make my health a priority.

6. I Found My True Identity

I grew confident of who I am as a follower of Christ (a loved and cared-for
child of God), who I belong to (my heavenly Father), about my eternal

destiny (with Him forever in heaven), and about my life having purpose. I developed this understanding from exposing myself to sound biblical teaching in church, in small group Bible studies, and through my own reading of the Scriptures. My heart and mind have been filled with these truths over the last three decades. This was a huge plus because it gave me a large reservoir to draw from. During these painful years I repeatedly read a list of statements I keep tucked away in my Bible. They had been the content of many prayers I had prayed for Reneé. Now they were as much for me. I needed to be reminded of them often. Two crucial ones were *I am complete in Christ and have all I need in Him* and *I can persevere and be victorious in any trial because of God's help and strength.*

Even today I continue to remind myself of these things. They make a huge difference during troubling times.

7. I Learned to Distinguish Between Truth and Lies

How? By focusing on the Word of God and being familiar with what it says. By avoiding negative, critical thinking that said God was indifferent or absent in my struggles. By knowing myself well enough to be aware of my limits, not kidding myself that I was superhuman. By realizing I couldn't do everything I had in the past and by enforcing wise, healthy boundaries (no more enabling or over-helping). By releasing the illusion that I had or needed control of Reneé or her circumstances. By accepting I wasn't perfect and that's okay. These things helped me detach from the trauma at hand and trust God with the outcome. I discovered I could care *for* my daughter without taking care *of* her.

8. I Made Time for Fun

I cultivated hobbies and tried new things. I gave myself permission to laugh again. It's all right. I know this idea sounds counterintuitive. Fun? Laughter? Delight? How can those be part of the horrific drama I'm going through every day? My friend, you need them. You need to balance hardship with lightheartedness. And just a little goes a long way.

Are you depleted with nothing left to give? Do you feel like a helpless victim? You don't have to anymore. Why not take a few minutes right now and talk with God before turning the page? Ask Him what He wants to say to you. He may direct you to choose one of these actions to incorporate, little by little, into your life. In time, you'll begin to cope better. In a few months, you'll feel a little stronger. This won't happen overnight, but if you take baby steps you can get there.

Scripture says, "In all their distress he too was distressed, and the angel of his presence saved them. In his love and mercy he redeemed them; he lifted them up and carried them" (Isaiah 63:9).

Your heavenly Father hurts with you.

He loves you with an eternal, unfailing love.

When you reach out to Him, He'll send help from His very presence to lift you up and carry you.

He'll make you strong so you can rebound from every trial.

Exhaustion. What's the remedy? Resilience.

You can be resilient.

Yes, you.

Scripture That Helps

Weeping may stay for the night, but rejoicing comes in the morning. **(Psalm 30:5)**

Therefore we do not lose heart. Though outwardly we are wasting away, yet inwardly we are being renewed day by day. **(2 Corinthians 4:16)**

11

A New Kind of Hope

We must accept finite disappointment, but never lose
infinite hope.

—Martin Luther King Jr.

Maybe your son or daughter was arrested—again. Her probation
was revoked. He got another DUI. She isn't married but she has a
child, maybe more than one. You've lost count how many times he's been
involuntarily committed in behavioral hospitals. She refuses to cooperate
with her treatment plan. He keeps going off his medication. She lost another job. She can't manage to get to work on time and is disrespectful to
the boss. He lost more money gambling. Unpaid debts are mounting. She
relapsed into her addiction for the umpteenth time. You longed for her to
stay clean and sober after that last stint in rehab. You thought this time it
was going to be different. Hope rose, then fell, shattered once more. Ugh.

Disappointments, setbacks, and blows like these can leave you worn
out and with your head down, your eyes glued to the ground in despair
and depression. You feel stuck in the mud. Each step takes monumental
effort. You plod through every day.

You may have reached a tipping point, a place where you can't believe
change is possible anymore. You want to have hope—oh, how you wish
you could—but you can't. You need a miracle. Could it happen?

Maybe you got your child back—several times—only to lose them
yet again to alcohol, to drugs, to mental illness, to a cult, to a hostile or

possessive boyfriend or girlfriend, to rebellion, to a life of crime, to one more bad decision, to any number of things. I wrote the following poem on one of my low days, trying to express my feelings.

Love: A Four-Letter Word
How we love our children,
But they've broken our hearts.
What was meant to bring joy became a portal to pain.
A highway to hell—another four-letter word;
A frightening carnival ride you can't get off.
A haunted house; a maze with no way out.
A hurricane with no eye of relief.
A wound that never heals.
Because we love them deeply, we suffer deeply.
When they break, we break.
Their tears stain our cheeks.
Their madness becomes our insanity.

Can we be honest? You aren't who you were before. You know more than you wish you did. You've been burned too many times. You may have become cynical, resentful, bitter. Is your faith wavering? Is your hope almost gone? Have you given up or are you about to?

I did, but God helped me find something I didn't know I needed. A better four-letter word than the hell or pain that love had brought: hope. A new kind of hope.

FRAGILE HOPE

Hope is one of those words we throw around loosely. We say, "I hope this job works out." "I hope I can go to the movies this weekend." "I hope I get to skydive." "I hope the car won't break down again." "I hope you like this gift." Hope is expecting or wishing for something you want to happen. It's yearning for a desire to come true. Hope is to trust in, wait for, or look for something or someone. It's to anticipate something good in the future.

As a child, I had many hopes. I grew up with a positive outlook on life. "High Hopes," a fifties song by Frank Sinatra, is a perfect example: "He's got high hopes, he's got high apple pie, in the sky hopes." That silly song encouraged me to believe the impossible might be possible if I didn't give up. Nice idea. In the struggle with my daughter, it felt unrealistic. What was I thinking?

Now, as a mother, for years I've held tightly to the hope that Reneé would be healed—physically, emotionally, and spiritually—no longer controlled by addiction, beaten down by mental health issues, devastated by cutting or by making unhealthy choices. My heart ached for her to live out the meaning of her name, to experience a rebirth and be made new. But my greatest hope was for Reneé to live and not die. What parent doesn't want that?

At times there would be great progress and answers to my prayers, then she would regress, and I did too. Seasons of waiting—dark valleys in which everything looked doomed to failure—were followed by glimmers of hope when my expectations peaked, only to nosedive once again. Quotes like Tertullian's "Hope is patience with the lamp lit" helped, but this roller-coaster ride grew wearisome. I had what you might call fragile hope.

Some of my hopes (actually many of them) had been dashed; others were shaky, weak, unrealistic, and impossible. How terribly discouraging.

I've come to realize that fragile hope focuses on half-truths we can't depend on, such as the following:

- *I trained my son in the Christian faith. I know he'll return to it.*
- *One day my daughter's going to be absolutely free from her addiction, mental-health issues, and self-injury. Those issues will never bother her again.*

- *If I believe and pray hard enough, my son won't experience negative or lifelong consequences from his choices. He won't get arrested, won't go to prison, won't get AIDS, and won't become an addict. Everything's going to be fine.*
- *God won't let my daughter die by suicide, an overdose, an accident, or some other tragic way. He wouldn't do that to me. After all, I've been faithful to Him all my life.*
- *My son is going to be reconciled to me because I believe it's going to happen.*
- *Someday I'll understand why. It will all make sense to me then.*

All these things could happen. But if we put all our hopes for our children in one basket—things working out the way we want—and they don't, what then? What if they're never free from bondage? What if reconciliation never comes? What if they never repent or change; they experience all the terrible consequences of their choices, and the unthinkable happens? There's a tension here.

The following things, however, we can know are true: God is all-powerful. He can do anything. He created the stars by the breath of His mouth. He made man from the dirt. Everything that exists does so because of His choosing, His sovereign will. He made each of us. He has full knowledge of the tiniest details of our lives: how many breaths we take each day, how many times our hearts skip a beat, the content of every passing thought. He's omnipotent, omniscient, omnipresent, omni-everything. What's impossible for Him? Nothing. He does miracles every day. I've heard innumerable stories of transformation. Maybe you have too. The Bible's full of them. God can even raise the dead.

> Then [the prophet Elijah] stretched himself out on the boy three times and cried out to the LORD, "LORD my God, let this boy's life return to him!"

The LORD heard Elijah's cry, and the boy's life returned to him, and he lived. Elijah picked up the child and carried him down from the room into the house. He gave him to his mother and said, "Look, your son is alive!" (1 Kings 17:21–23)

"Lazarus, come out!" The dead man came out, his hands and feet wrapped with strips of linen, and a cloth around his face. (John 11:43–44)

I believe these aren't myths or fables. These stories are real. They were recorded and handed down over the centuries to build our faith. We need this kind of hope. God's the author. He's Lord of the impossible. He's in the life-changing business. It's the reason He entered our dark, broken world in the person of Jesus.

But there's a dilemma: another person's free will is involved. We have no control over anyone else's choices. We have to let go of the dream that one day everything will resolve neatly, with a pretty bow on top, that our sons will be restored, that our daughters will come to their senses, that our prayers for repentance and renewal will be answered.

In God's eyes our wayward children are like disoriented sheep. Sadly, not all lost sheep want to be found. Some prefer the open range. They can be pretty clueless about their need for rescue. They refuse help, refuse correction, refuse direction, and refuse to listen or respond to their Master's voice calling them to come home. Everyone isn't healed. Not everyone will get a happy ending. Some of our children will be overcome by their struggles and weaknesses.

We need to believe the following:

There is no medicine like hope, no incentive so great, no tonic so powerful as expectations of something better tomorrow.
—Orison Swett Marden, physician and author

You can live forty days without food, seven days without water, and seven minutes without air, but you can't live a moment without hope. —Celebrate Recovery

These are good statements and I like them, but in my opinion, we need a different kind of hope. One that's not contingent on another person's choices. One that's not demanding. A firm one based on what's true, unchangeable, and unbreakable.

FIRM HOPE

Firm hope focuses on solid truths we can depend on from God's Word. Here are examples of firm hope:

- God loves and cares more about our children than we do. He will never stop seeking them (2 Samuel 7:14–15).
- God is in control no matter how things may appear. He's our ally, not our adversary. We may not always understand what He allows, but we choose to trust Him because He's trustworthy (Jeremiah 29:11).
- God will be with us in *everything* we go through. We are never alone. He's with our children too. We don't need to be afraid of anything (Deuteronomy 31:8).
- Nothing can separate us from the love of God. It's unfailing and eternal (Romans 8:38–39).
- God will give strength and courage for the journey, wherever it takes us and no matter what happens. He'll provide for every trial, even the valley of the shadow of death. When we're weak and weary, He'll make us resilient (Philippians 4:13; Psalm 23:4, ESV).
- God will use our greatest weaknesses and failures for His glory. He can restore and redeem even the most painful experiences we're walking in (Psalm 71:20).

What does this mean? How does He do it? The answer to this question fleshes out what firm hope looks like. For me, it's believing that God won't waste our pain.

- He can use it for good in our lives.
- He can use it to help us become the person He wants us to be. It doesn't change His plans or purposes for our lives.
- He can use it to draw us into deeper intimacy with Him, to make us more like His Son. Suffering is His primary tool to chisel away what isn't like Christ. He can use it to enhance our relationships with the people He's put in our lives, deepening and strengthening them.
- He can use it to help others, even though we may never know about it.
- He can use it to speak to our hearts and teach us more about Himself, things we never knew before and couldn't know any other way (Jeremiah 33:3).
- There's always a purpose for our pain. Always (2 Corinthians 1:3–4, 6; I'll speak more about this in the next chapter).

SUFFERING ISN'T ALL BAD

"We've bought the lie that suffering is a mistake," wrote Kara Tippetts, "but [suffering is the place] where you see how absolutely needy you are for Jesus, and that neediness is a good thing. The broken places in our life are the places that really draw us close to God."[22]

Can we be like the three men described in Daniel 3:17–18? You may be familiar with the story. It's always fascinated me. About to be thrown into a red-hot furnace, certain death, they boldly affirmed, "The God we serve is able to deliver us from it, and he will deliver us from Your Majesty's hand. But even if he does not, we want you to know . . . we will not serve your gods or worship the image of gold you have set up."

That's it.

This should be our goal: faith that proclaims "Even if He does not . . ." Even if my child never changes, I will still trust the Lord with all the unknowns, the unanswered questions, and the mysteries. If my suffering allows me to see my spiritual neediness and causes me to be closer to God, then good can come from it.

But none of us is perfect. Some days we feel strong in our faith, on others not so much. In our humanity we still struggle. I sure do. Our journey tends to be up and down, but our Father understands, He knows our hearts and puts no pressure on us to *do it right* all the time with our child. We do that to ourselves. He gives us grace. Lots of it. I hope you'll decide not to throw away your faith like some disheartened parents have.

Our prayers may take a long time to be answered. The waiting and not knowing could consume us and make us miserable. Maybe that's happened to you in the past, but this can gradually change. How? When your hope is rooted in God alone, trusting Him in the furnace with the what and the how and the when of the working out of His plan.

A dear friend often reminds me, "As long as our child is still breathing, there's still hope." How comforting her words are. Let God be the hope of your heart. Norman Wright noted, "You may not be there yet. Your child may still be wandering. It may seem like forever. And for some, it could be. . . . But never, never give up hope."[23]

In my journey to trust God for Reneé, my focus shifted. I realized I needed to hunger more for Him, even more than I wanted her to be whole and well. My waiting and longing exposed my real need. It wasn't for *someone else* to change but for *me* to change—the only one I had any real power over. It took several years of working on my own recovery before this need for a shift became clear.

Reneé helped me see it one day when I asked, "How can I help you the most right now?" I expected a list of practical things I could do to help her stay strong in her recovery, but her answer surprised me. And she was right on. "I need you to keep working on *your own* recovery. I can tell when you are and it helps me so much, Mom." I was speechless. How wise. She put the focus back on me, where it belonged. What an eye-opening moment.

What changes did I need to make? I needed to be less controlling and fearful, complain less, worry less, and give thanks more. To not be so consumed with Reneé's welfare, but pull back emotionally and give attention to my own self-care. To be honest with God and draw closer to Him. Accept my weaknesses. Forgive myself. Grieve the losses. Admit I was powerless. Surrender my dreams and let go of what I wanted. That's plenty to keep me busy for a long time.

God gently led me to see that my daughter may never want to change. To insist or try to force her to do so would only make her—and me—miserable. Instead, I needed to work on myself, the only one I could do something about. And I needed God to help me do it.

The most important thing about my life wasn't how my children were doing (as important as that was) but my relationship with Jesus, my Savior. That's what really mattered most. What's the most important thing about your life? Do you want it to change? It can if you want it to. When I chose to focus on Christ, my real hope, firm hope, was revealed.

Firm hope is based on the character and nature of God, on who He is and what He's done for us in His Son and what He says He'll do in the future. These truths make this kind of hope certain, unchangeable, secure, steady, and strong. This kind of hope is rooted in His life and promises, in His infallible, living Word. That's what makes it firm.

Our challenge is to loosen our grip on the fragile hopes we've been setting our hearts on. They're slippery and elusive. They slip through our fingers like sand. We need to live by faith as we come before the King of kings with open-handed trust, willing to receive whatever He allows, like the three men in the furnace.

Did you know the Bible contains over seven thousand promises? When we're more familiar with them (at least a portion of them), it will help us build a better hope, one that's strong enough to stand on when the next crisis comes. And it *will* come because that's life in this world. But the giver of these promises is our helper. He's the eternal, dependable promise keeper: "The LORD is trustworthy in all he promises and faithful in all he does" (Psalm 145:13).

Hope is the rope thrown to us by almighty God, who fastens it tightly around our waists to keep us from falling into a pit of despair. It's His work, not ours. He's the One who makes us resilient: "And the God of all grace, who called you to his eternal glory in Christ, after you have suffered a little while, will himself restore you and make you strong, firm and steadfast" (1 Peter 5:10).

Restored. Strong. Firm. Steadfast. I love hearing that.

After more than ten years of struggling, I now believe with confidence that God has a better hope for us. If we let Him, He'll help us stop clinging to the desire for our kids to become everything we dreamed they could be. We can trust Him with our broken dreams and fragile hopes. He'll give us new ones. Our children may not have the career we thought they would, but they'll be alive. There may not be a wedding to plan or grandchildren to enjoy, but there will be other joys and achievements to celebrate in our own lives. The Enemy will try to trip us up by telling us lies. *You weren't good enough. This is all your fault. You should have been smarter, stricter, wiser. You could've done a better job. You failed.* We can't live like that any longer. The goals we had for our sons and daughters were good, but they were our goals, not theirs.

Dear Mom or Dad, please take hold of this new kind of hope. This is where your strength lies. God is present in your pain. Focus on Him, on what He's done for you, on what He's doing in you now. Don't believe the lies of the Enemy. God will raise you up from the ash heap, and in His timing show you His purposes for your suffering. Then you'll see it wasn't all bad.

Today, I'm holding on to this new kind of hope for what almighty God can do in me and not solely for Reneé. My stormy years haven't been wasted. By focusing on truth and becoming more resilient, I've learned to ride the crest of the waves—most of the time. I'm quicker than I used to be to find the balance of being in the pain yet above it. More often my hope shifts onto the solid ground of His eternal, unchanging promises. When answers delay and the waiting gets long with no resolution in sight, I have an enlarged confidence that my Father is working out His good plan for me. "Blessed is the one who trusts in the LORD, whose confidence is in him" (Jeremiah 17:7). His Word is true. His hope is real. His purposes will prevail. He's making my broken places beautiful, more than I could've imagined.

A struggling mom once told me, "My earthly hopes revealed my heavenly hopes!" I wholeheartedly agree. We've both learned to let go of what we previously desired—not that we don't want those things anymore. Now we know with more confidence than ever before that God alone is our hope, our help, our life, our peace, our deliverer, our strength-giver, and our comforter.

A Prayer for Hope

My prayer for you is that your hope will be the kind that's spoken of in Romans 15:13: "May the God of hope fill you with all joy and peace as you trust in him, so that you may overflow with hope by the power of the Holy Spirit."

I pray that you experience

- enduring peace as you walk your difficult path
- unshakable faith that whatever comes you'll be confident God will see you through
- divine strength that far surpasses your own to carry you through everything that comes into your life
- unspeakable joy that defies reason and an ability to be thankful in any circumstance because you know the living God is your constant companion

- supernatural ability to trust no matter what you see happening in your loved one's life
- willingness to accept disillusionment and let God bring you to a place of contentment, assured of His great love for you and your child.

Are you stuck focusing on what isn't happening in your child's life? On your dissatisfaction, disappointments, and shattered dreams? Or on what could happen in yours? You get to choose.

"Two men looked out from prison bars; One saw the mud, the other saw the stars."[24] One saw his dismal position; the other saw his opportunities.

Where are you looking? The mud or the stars? Reneé would encourage you to look up. To remember the stars.[25]

Scripture That Helps

So we fix our eyes not on what is seen, but on what is unseen, since what is seen is temporary, but what is unseen is eternal. (2 Corinthians 4:18)

I remember my affliction and my wandering, the bitterness and the gall. I well remember them, and my soul is downcast within me. Yet this I call to mind and therefore I have hope: Because of the LORD's great love we are not consumed, for his compassions never fail. They are new every morning; great is your faithfulness. (Lamentations 3:19–23)

12

The Why Question: Finding Purpose for the Pain

This is the purpose of our lives. . . . To let the light of Christ shine through the dark moments as well as in the glory days when everything is wonderful.

—Sheila Walsh, *Life Is Tough but God Is Faithful*

Why would God let this happen? What could be the reason? This makes no sense to me. What good can come from this? I've asked questions like these many times over the years. You probably have too. When tragedies occur, one of the first things we do is ask why, as though someone could have an answer.

Can purpose really come from pain and suffering? I wanted it to, but there were many days I wasn't so sure.

The belief that purpose can come from pain isn't natural or automatic. We tend to pull away from the suggestion the same way we recoil from anything that hurts.

When I was young I was a crybaby. The slightest scratch caused me to wail with gusto. My parents would come running in a panic, certain I'd broken a bone. I'm better now, but I still don't like pain. Most people try to avoid being hurt as much as possible. It's to be expected.

As human beings, our goal is typically to escape what could injure or harm us. No one in their right mind enjoys being hurt. The idea that we could find purpose in or from pain intrigues us. The sheer possibility is alluring. Oh, how we want it to be true. Count me in.

As I've brought my pain to God and struggled to make sense of it, I've seen that most meaningful transformations come about as a direct result of hard experiences. Childbirth and labor pains bring forth life. Children lose baby teeth to gain larger adult ones. The discipline of exercise tears down muscles to build them back up stronger. Another great example is found in the essence of the gospel: good has come to all mankind as a result of the sufferings of Christ. The Crucifixion was followed by the Resurrection. That's huge purpose from pain.

Why do tragedies happen, especially the ones we're facing now? Why does God let bad things happen to good people? Why does He remain silent? Why doesn't He answer our prayers? I don't know.

Are you taken aback by what appears to be a lack of God's concern? Do you wonder if the suffering of His people matters to Him? "Can't He do something?" we ask. "How can He just stand by and watch? Does He really care? Is this situation with my child punishment for my doing something wrong? Are there no more miracles? Is there no more mercy? Has God run out of power to help? Did His well run dry?"

I wondered too.

WHYS WEAR ME OUT!

In the beginning, I wanted—no, I *needed*—answers to understand why all those terrible things happened to my daughter . . . and to me. All the whys made me weary. Long days and endless nights were full of tortured speculation. To be honest, sometimes I still wonder. It's so hard to make sense of it. I scratch my head in bewilderment.

Our questions aren't new. People have been asking them for centuries, whenever the circumstances of life became miserable and unexplainable or when God (as they understood Him) didn't do what they thought

He should have done. "If God is so loving and good, then how could He let this happen?" Can we agree with Job, who suffered terribly though he did nothing wrong, "What? Shall we receive only pleasant things from the hand of God and never anything unpleasant?" (Job 2:10, TLB). What purpose could be in those unpleasant things?

Let's cut to the chase. My answer to these tough questions is quite simple: I believe difficult things happen because of what transpired in the beginning of human history. God's first two children, Adam and Eve, were given the gift of free will. They had the freedom to choose whether or not they would obey what their maker said: "You must not eat from the tree of the knowledge of good and evil, for when you eat from it you will certainly die" (Genesis 2:17).

They thought they knew better, that God was holding out on them. They wanted more, so they took fruit from the forbidden tree and ate. The rest is history, literally, His-story. After that event, everything in the created world was broken, fallen. Sin entered into what had been a perfect environment and brought with it decay, rebellion, strife, destruction, and death. Look what happened to the first family. In the beginning, Adam and Eve had two sons (that Scripture names), and one murdered the other. What a tragedy. They not only lost one son through a tragic event, but they also had to grieve the fact that it was their firstborn who caused their pain. Is it any wonder the world is full of so much suffering today?

Every living thing decays: animals, plants, and people get diseases, age, and die. Flowers wilt and fade. Hair grays even in the animal kingdom. Skin wrinkles. Bones break. Hearing fades. Eyes dim. Hearts stop. Our world is full of natural disasters, not to mention famines, disease epidemics, wars, and rumors of wars. Marriages end. Relationships fall apart. Cancer strikes innocent children. Terrorists bomb. Soldiers lose limbs. Teenagers stray. Babies are aborted. Hatred, prejudice, injustice, and violence exist in every corner of the globe.

In our cases, beloved children become addicts or alcoholics and destroy themselves. Mental illness disables. Self-injurers mutilate. Eating disorders damage. Prisons overflow. HIV and AIDS impair. Precious princesses run away. Hearts break. And sometimes it's too much. We become disillusioned and lose our faith.

But I refuse to let go of mine. That you're reading this book tells me you're still clinging to your faith too. Do you still believe, as I do, that God is all-powerful and can do anything? I believe He's present everywhere and misses nothing. I believe He makes no mistakes, isn't cruel, and doesn't overlook my (or your) problems. I believe He hears every prayer. I also believe He's good—all the time. He loves us and He cares about our pain far more than we're capable of comprehending.

Though the world's first parents invited sin and pain into the world, God is not crippled by their mistake. There is always purpose beyond the pain.

Don't Blame God

In *When God Doesn't Make Sense,* Dr. James Dobson, founder of Focus on the Family and Family Talk, presented a profound and helpful response that I read when I was grappling with these critical questions: "God usually does not choose to answer those questions in this life! . . . He will not parade His plans and purposes for our approval. We must never forget that He is God. As such He wants us to believe and trust in Him despite the things we don't understand. It's that straightforward."[26]

He continued, "Some of us need to forgive God for those heartaches that are charged to His account. You've carried resentment against Him for years. Now it's time to let go of it. . . . Then ask His forgiveness for our lack of faith. It's called reconciliation."[27] I interpreted Dobson to mean that if we're holding a grudge against God, even though He didn't do anything to need to be forgiven, we may need to say the words for our own benefit. I talked about this in chapter 8 on forgiveness.

In another attempt to make sense of suffering, Max Lucado wrote, "Don't blame suffering in the world on the anger of God. He's not mad;

he didn't mess up. Follow our troubles to their headwaters, and you won't find an angry or befuddled God. But you will find a sovereign God. . . . Your pain has a purpose. Your problems, struggles, heartaches, and hassles cooperate toward one end—the glory of God."[28]

And God Himself says, "Trust me in your times of trouble, so I can rescue you and you can give me glory" (Psalm 50:15, TLB).

It's challenging to make sense out of our trials, especially when they involve our beloved children. More like Adam and Eve than I wanted to admit, I thought God had made a big mistake. I wanted only pleasant things. I wanted more. Are you like me?

FASCINATING TRAGEDIES FROM SCRIPTURE

John 9:1–3 tells a story about a man blind from birth. Jesus's disciples tried to make sense out of this tragedy. Like me, they were asking hard questions with no satisfying explanations. And like me, they wanted—no, they *needed*—answers. Whose fault was his blindness? Why did that happen? And (to bring it home for you and me) why are we the parents of troubled sons and daughters?

The disciples received an unexpected reply: "This happened so that the works of God might be displayed in him" (verse 3). Whoa. Is it possible He might give the same answer to us?

Is your response like mine? *Sorry, Jesus, but I'd rather make You look good some other way, one that doesn't hurt so much. I'll pass on the pain and take only the good, easy things, please. I'm not sure I want that kind of purpose. Can't we make a deal? Work something else out? Come on!*

Another baffling story in the New Testament is about a man named Lazarus (John 11:1–44). Maybe you remember it. He got sick and died. But wait, he was a close friend of Rabbi Jesus, not a casual acquaintance. His sisters sent for their good friend to come, but He didn't. Because of His delay, the unthinkable happened. Their beloved brother breathed his last and ended up in a tomb.

What did they do wrong? Didn't Jesus care? If He did, then why in the world did He let that happen? It caused them intense grief. He could have saved Lazarus with a word from where He was. Was this some sort of punishment or cruel joke? They had no clue.

Listen closely to the words of the Son of God when He did arrive: "This sickness is not to end in death, but for the glory of God, so that the Son of God may be glorified by it" (John 11:4, NASB).

Lazarus got sick in order to shine a spotlight on God.

Brokenhearted Mom or Dad, I propose that if you have a child in turmoil, maybe, just maybe, it's to do the same. Maybe your pain exists, at least in part, for His glory?

THE TREASURES OF DARKNESS

Another possible reason for our heartache could be explained in this verse: "I will give you the treasures of darkness and hidden wealth of secret places" (Isaiah 45:3, NASB). God has hidden something special for us to find in our suffering: treasure. It's a little like geocaching,[29] only far better. Is it possible He allowed Lazarus to suffer and die to send him on a treasure hunt? I believe that's what happened to me. My journey out of the ashes of broken dreams turned into exactly that. It was both unexpected and unwanted. However, unlike geocaching, it didn't sound like any fun. I didn't want to go. Did you?

But we don't have a choice, do we? We have to go. I went, reluctantly of course, but what treasures I found! I've shared many of them with you in this book. But the greatest prize was the richness of my relationship with the Prince of Peace Himself, the Faithful One whose love never fails, the Hope of Glory in whom we rejoice. I'd already known Him since I was a teen, but I came to know Him as never before. Recently I heard another hurting mom say there were few things that could take you to a level of brokenness and utter dependence on God like the pain of having something go desperately wrong with your child. She's right, but

I discovered He would never disappoint me: "Those who hope in me will not be disappointed" (Isaiah 49:23).

Jesus is my treasure. Who or what is yours?

I discovered He was right in the middle of the painful parenting journey I couldn't make sense of.

There were plenty of times I wondered where God was, but He never let me down. He showed up in so many places. His unexplainable peace would come. In my weakest hours, when I didn't think I could endure the situation with Reneé any longer, just enough strength and courage were given for the moment. He helped me stand solidly on the things I could know for sure, the firm hopes mentioned in the last chapter, and I found they sustained me. Scripture verses I'd been familiar with for a long time would suddenly come alive in fresh, new ways, providing what was needed for that day. Breakthroughs came at the right time. A song on the radio, a comment someone would say, a card or an e-mail would bring a comforting message perfect for my heart. Likewise, God provided for all our needs: financial, emotional, spiritual, practical. What beautiful ways caring people helped, encouraged, and walked with me in the mess. People showed up and loved us, and Reneé, well.

You can find this to be true in your own life by holding on to your faith and not walking away from God. Don't give up because you don't understand what's happening or because the pain is too deep. Choose to keep trusting. Stay. He's there and He cares even though you see no evidence of this truth. When you can't see Him or feel Him, persevere anyway. Persist in your faith and spiritual disciplines. Go to church, pray, and don't shut your Bible in anger. Continue bringing yourself to this Living Text. He wants to meet you there. Keep putting yourself in situations and places where He can speak to you. You can also find other nontraditional, creative ways to connect with your Maker. Being outside in nature is a great way. Go to the beach or the mountains, a park, a lake, a river. Look at the clouds in the sky by day or the moon and stars by night. Take a walk. Ride a bike. Listen to beautiful, relaxing music while sitting in your backyard. Each of these can help you feel closer to the lover of your soul. We all have our unique preferences. I like to walk, especially on the beach, and look at the sky. Tom likes the mountains and listening to smooth jazz.

How have you seen God in your journey? Take a moment to reflect and remember.

I knew God could use my pain for His glory, but I couldn't imagine how. Grief's fog was too thick for a long time for me to see the larger picture, but He kept working in me. Little by little, as I recovered and grew stronger, I was finally ready to ask, "What do You want me to do with this, Lord?" instead of only asking *why* it happened. But it took a while. Years.

Kara Tippetts discovered that "when you come to the end of yourself, that's when something else can begin."[30] A pastor's wife and mom of four, she wrote authentically about her journey with terminal cancer.[31]

As Tom and I saw our healing progress, something began to stir in our hearts. We found ourselves connecting more and more with other parents in similar situations, desperate for someone to talk to who could understand and offer words of encouragement instead of platitudes or "just pray" solutions. As a result, we met still more hurting moms and dads. Before I knew it, this became my passion: to encourage parents with broken hearts by helping them find strength to cope when their children were in turmoil. It gave a great deal of purpose for my own pain. Since I didn't know where to turn for help when I began this arduous journey, it was tremendously meaningful to be able to offer it to others. It got me up in the morning and kept me going on my roughest days. It's one of the treasures I found in the darkness.

But I have a sneaking suspicion some of you feel inadequate. You're thinking negatively about yourselves. *Who am I to try and help other hurting parents?* It's not our talent or ability that matters. God uses those who are faithful, available, and willing to venture into new territory. This is what He wants for each of His followers: willingness and humble dependence. When you feel ready, you can discover your own treasures by asking God what He's taught you on your journey. If you journal, look back over your writings to recall the new discoveries you've made. Think back and notice positive ways in which you've grown and changed. Can you recognize any gains or benefits for your soul? These are some of your treasures. At some point you may want to ask, *Lord, what do You want me to do with this?*

Carol Kent wrote in *A New Kind of Normal,*

> Unexpected circumstances mean life will never be the same as it once was.
>
> Instead of running away or withdrawing to a prison of their own making, they choose to embrace the new opportunities and unexpected joys that can only be known by those who say:
>
> I will survive.
> I will persevere.
> I will be vulnerable.
> I will forgive.
> I will trust.
> I will hold those I love with open hands.
> I will be thankful.
> I will choose purposeful action.[32]

Let's get back to those tough questions: Why did this happen? Why weren't my prayers answered? Was it a lack of faith? Was it my fault? Wasn't God listening? Doesn't He care?

Indeed He was listening. He does care. If you're trusting in Him, nothing is wrong with your faith. It isn't your fault. But He may have higher plans for you. It will demand solid confidence in a sovereign God who doesn't always tell us why on this side of heaven.

God, in His wisdom and mercy, allows us to experience trials so we will reflect Him in our struggle. Could people be strengthened by your struggles? Maybe He's calling you to something new, as He did with us. It could be dangerous and involve risk. It might be an exciting, once-in-a-lifetime adventure. This is what a life fully surrendered to God can be.

But there's more.

When we do our best to make Him seen, we have the opportunity to be like Lazarus when he "paraded the power of Jesus down the Main Street of his world. . . . [He] selected to suffer for God's glory. His light prisms through their aching lives and spills forth in a cascade of colors. God-glimpses."[33] *Wow. I see it now.* That's what we can be: prisms of God's radiant, majestic light. We can give those in need all around us a fresh view of their Creator. We, too, can be God-glimpses.

Our greatest pain can become our greatest passion. God can take the messiest parts of our lives and turn them into miracles for others. Our trials occur for the sake of God and His glory. It's not about me or you. It's all about Him, the Lord of glory.

Is It Time to Turn Pain into Purpose?

What about you, dear Mom or Dad? When you feel ready and have given yourself time to heal by processing your experiences and feelings, will you let God use you? Will you let Him use you while you hurt and wait? While you pray for your child to come to their senses and come home? While you hold on to hope and choose to trust even in the face of the frightening unknown? If you're willing—and only if you're past the exhausting, overwhelming part of your journey—you can reach out your hand to someone else in pain. You don't need to have your act together or know all the answers. You can encourage someone else in ways you never imagined. As weak as you may feel, you can be a God prism.

- You can find purpose in your pain.
- You can grow personally and gain a better understanding of your strengths and weaknesses.
- You can grow closer to God.

- You can be strengthened in your faith, your character developed.
- You can learn to endure hardships.
- You can offer comfort to others.

My husband likes to say, "God doesn't transform us in isolation, but in community, in the context of the body of Christ. He never intended that we keep the good things He's done for us to ourselves, but instead, to use them to serve others." I think he's right.

It's up to you. But let me add a little caveat here: if you're barely making it through each day and need all your energy to deal with your child's issues, then focus on that. Please be kind to yourself first. *Don't* feel you have to add to your burden by pushing yourself into some kind of ministry. If God wants you to touch others, He'll let you know when and how.

Scripture That Helps

The LORD will fulfill his purpose for me. (Psalm 138:8, ESV)

But thanks be to God, who always leads us in triumph in Christ, and manifests through us the sweet aroma of the knowledge of Him in every place. (2 Corinthians 2:14, NASB)

13

Can You
Thrive Again?

When we have children, we know they will need us,
and maybe love us, but we don't have a clue how hard
it is going to be.

—Anne Lamott, Salon.com

Can you picture yourself thriving again? What do you think—really? Maybe you believe it's too late for you. You've languished in the desert too long. Your soul has turned brown and withered up like an autumn leaf, beaten down like an old workhorse. Stunted. Could you be rejuvenated and returned to a flourishing condition? Could you feel fully alive again, rise above the trial, be the healthy person you once were before all this happened?

During the worst times with Reneé, my goal was simply to survive. I'm sure you've experienced many circumstances in your life where you felt that way: an illness, the death of a loved one, a financial setback, a divorce, a miserable job, a loved one's battle with cancer or another life-threatening illness, a test of your physical endurance like a runner's race, maybe a marathon. The idea of being able to flourish again in this situation with my daughter never entered my mind. Not even close. If you would have said such a thing was possible, I would have laughed in your face and said, "Are you crazy?"

You may feel like that right now. You're worn out. The mere suggestion of thriving is preposterous in the early days, months, and years of the journey, when you feel as though your heart's been pulverized.

Many of the things I've shared in the previous chapters build on each other, gaining momentum to help you move toward a goal—to thrive again. I've hinted at the possibility several times. Like a thousand-piece jigsaw puzzle, each little shape has an intended place, a crucial part to play in the bigger picture. Imagine you're putting together your personal recovery puzzle, assembling it into your very own, unique picture of overall health and wholeness. What would it look like?

Have you wondered what other hurting parents have done? What does their recovery puzzle look like? I wondered too. I wanted to know so that maybe, just maybe, I could survive myself.

Last week I asked a handful of seasoned parents, veterans on the journey from a broad cross-section of situations, the following question: How did you come to thrive again? What did you do? What did it look like specifically?

Here's what they had to say, just for you.

- "I don't blame myself for the poor choices my children made, and I don't take credit for their good choices, either. I spend my energy praying for them and living a healthy life myself. I hope my prayers and the way I live will lead them to peace and back to God."

- "[I came to thrive again] by coming to grips with the sovereignty of God in light of His character: That He is great, good, trustworthy, wise, able, and loving. I needed to decide what I believed about God and then allow that to speak to my circumstances, rather than the other way around—allowing the circumstances to drive what I believed about Him. Good theology was so important. I had to believe He was as big as my pain and fear. Bigger. Then I looked for His hand moving where I could see it while I learned to trust Him again when I couldn't see Him moving readily in my child's life. It's not anything I did. It was God."

- "One thing that helped me tremendously was attending family therapy with my husband and son at his rehab program. We learned many communication skills under the care of his therapist. It also helped to hear her praise our son for the decisions he was making to pursue his recovery. We might not have taken them seriously had we not had her perspective. And our son had the chance to hear from his therapist and from us how we had been affected by his addiction. We learned a mutual appreciation and respect for each other in those sessions.

  "It has been critical in helping me maintain my focus on God's character and promises. Involvement in my neighborhood Bible study also helped keep me dependent on God's Word and in community with other women. It helped to know they were praying specifically for me and my family. And it also gives me the opportunity to be involved in their lives: praying for their needs, hosting the study from time to time, and serving them (bringing meals when someone's had a surgery, for example). That takes my eyes off of me and my challenges."

- "I am trusting God by faith in this difficult place, accepting for now the hurting heart that I carry with me every day over my children. Even as I write, tears well up in my eyes.

  "I've had to learn to rest completely in God and His Word. I actually became even hungrier for His Word, because I needed its comfort and needed my relationship strengthened with the Lord. My kids needed Him too. But if my relationship wasn't strong enough, what would happen if they came back to me ready for Him and I had grown weak?

"I do not have any answers, I just have a God who is a great comforter and who is enough. I rest in His sovereignty!

"I would tell you to trust Him to be enough, to draw closer with your spouse as you draw close to God, and to stay in His Word and in His church. We need to do these no matter what our life is like."

- "Placing my bipolar son completely in God's hands was difficult for me. I would do it and then take back the burden and responsibility for saving him from his own destructive patterns. It began to crush me, as you can imagine. One day I read the account of Hagar and Ishmael in Genesis 21, how she placed her baby under the bush and turned her back on him, thinking he would die. But God heard her cry and he lived. That day, almost five years ago, I placed my boy under the bush and into God's care. Since that time, when I am tempted to take on the burden of keeping my son alive and healthy, I remind myself he is under the bush with God. While there have been challenges, I know my son is in the best care, and I am now able to love him where he is. I am relaxed and thriving."

- "Being in community with other hurting parents whose journey with their prodigal child did not typify my own helped me thrive again. This diversity of experience helped me maintain a balanced perspective. Reaching out to other parents helped me remember how much of a role others have played in my own story. As the mother of a gay son, I made the most of any opportunities to get to know his friends. Fear was my first big battle. This hands-on education, not just from books, helped me thrive again too. I discovered my stereotypes were much worse than the actual, living, breathing human beings. Doing this helped answer some of my questions and took the edge off my greatest fear, which was that my son would be convinced by the gay community that we couldn't love him unconditionally."

- "Over the last few months I've had an epiphany: I cannot change my addict. I cannot keep him from feeding his addiction, whether it is with drugs, alcohol, or other behaviors. There are two or three actions that have helped me realize I can only monitor and change myself.

  "My husband and I started a Nar-Anon group in our community. Sharing with other families and hearing their struggles empowers me. I find our situation isn't as dire as someone else's and take comfort in the realization. I hear a mother tell how she told her son, 'You can no longer live here. I can't stop you from using, but I can stop you from doing it in my home.' From her I draw strength to face tough decisions.

  "A second action that helps me thrive is posting daily encouraging messages for other hurting parents on social media. These are scriptures that remind me of the hope I have in Christ and they inspire me to share the comfort with which I've been comforted—verses planted deep in my heart that are pulled out during trying times. By typing out these scriptures, I'm reminded of the breadth, depth, and width of God's love for me and my addict.

  "The third action was realizing it's time for me to live outside the shadow of addiction. I've wasted so many years living in fear of the what-ifs that I missed out on the world around me. No more. My husband and I bought a travel trailer and have begun a new adventure."

- "I stayed connected to God through the hard and painful times by taking walks at night and pouring my heart out in prayer to Him, finding beauty in creation, giving praise and thanks to Him for these gifts, and reading scriptures and discerning the insights I gained from them, especially passages in Genesis and Isaiah. These insights included the following:

- Perfect parenting is not a guarantee of children following the Lord.
- God knows and understands how I feel having a rebellious child.
- God is my ally, not my adversary, in this painful journey.
- Jesus sympathizes with our weakness (Hebrews 4:14–16).
- Jesus ever lives to make intercession for us (Hebrews 7:25).
- The Holy Spirit intercedes for us (Romans 8:26–27).
- God comforts us (2 Corinthians 1:3–4).

"Another thing that helped me thrive was attending Al-Anon and another support group just for parents. They helped me learn about addiction and trauma in a safe community and to process my feelings there."

- "I finally realized how empty I'd become. There was no refilling myself anymore. When my daughter moved out, I began to heal. My happiness and joy aren't dependent on her anymore, but I still ache for her. I pray there's help out there for her and that she'll take it. I realized I couldn't run her life anymore, but I need reminders once in a while since I'm a recovering codependent."
- "Engage in what is happening and educate yourself by reading up on the varying subjects your child is affected by.

In our case that included mental illness education through the National Alliance on Mental Illness (NAMI) and books on parenting prodigal children (including homosexual behavior).

"Joyce Meyer's teachings and books also helped tremendously. I focused on those that taught positive, godly thinking and controlling my mind to always look on the bright side.

"I also read a lot of books on grief and mourning. I allowed myself to imagine worse-case scenarios in a logical, controlled way so I would not be blindsided by a bad turn of events. By doing that, things always looked brighter.

"All of this has helped me grow into a better, stronger, more compassionate and less judgmental person, so I suppose you could look at this as a fertilizer to my growth that has allowed me to thrive again."

- "After accepting that our children were not going to become what we had imagined, I decided to become what I wanted for myself, to think about my own dreams for me and not the dreams I had for my children. I realized I had done all I could and needed to hand them over to the care of God, let them fly alone, and get out of the way so they could own all of their decisions, both good and bad.

"I detached and accepted they have their own life to live. They don't owe me anything and I can't expect anything from them.

"I don't initiate contact with my children unless it's absolutely necessary (a death in the family, important mail addressed to them and received at our house, and so on). When they initiate contact, I only address the issues they ask about. This way they tell me whatever they feel like telling me and I share with them about my life. I don't ask any questions about their life. By doing this, I respect their boundaries and mind my own business.

"Honestly, it's been a very long process, and so much of it had to do with continually releasing our kids to God, going to the worst-case scenario, and telling Him even that was okay. The crazy-maker is that as I offered my children up to God, it was the only thing that gave me peace. It meant I was applying faith to each of them. As my husband always says, 'The greatest equation in the Bible is Trials plus Faith equals Life (resurrection power).'"

Are you barely making it, crawling through each day? Do you feel like your heart and soul have shriveled up? Has your spiritual well gone dry? Consider the words of the prophet Malachi: "But for you who revere my name, the sun of righteousness will rise with healing in its rays. And you will go out and frolic like well-fed calves" (4:2). This could be you.

You can flourish again. If the parents who offered their insights in this chapter can, and if I can, then as you gradually begin to do the things we did, one day you can too.

In 1980 a volcano erupted on Mount St. Helens in Washington. Fifty-seven people died. Mass destruction to wildlife and the landscape spread over a hundred miles. Everything in the path of the lava flow, hot gases, and debris was destroyed. Only ashes and charred rubble were left behind. No signs of life appeared to remain. Yet some plants and animals survived. Life did not entirely end. Astonishingly, less than a month after the eruption, avalanche lilies began to bloom. In time, insects scurried about. Slowly, miraculously, over three decades, the mountain and the surrounding area have revived. The forest and wildlife thrive once again. Now that's something to marvel over, isn't it?

Take a moment to look back over this chapter. Do you see a few things you think you could do to begin to revive yourself? Choose one. Write it down and ask God to help you begin.

Take these words to heart.

Like Mount St. Helens, you can thrive again.

Scripture That Helps

I will sing a new song to you, my God; . . . I will make music to you, to the One who gives victory. (Psalm 144:9–10)

14

Discoveries About Prayer

In retrospect, I see that God in loving kindness and faithfulness never let me go. He brought me through by His grace alone and through my parents' daily prayers for me.

—A Former Prodigal

When you're in deep emotional pain over your child, it can affect every area of your life. Maybe you've been a strong Christian, faithfully reading your Bible, spending time in prayer daily for years. That was me. Having been a pastor's wife for more than fourteen years and then a missionary for almost fifteen, some would say I was a professional at this stuff, right? Wrong. During my dark times with Renée, I couldn't think straight. I couldn't make sense of all that had happened. I never felt more inadequate. Praying for her became more and more difficult as the years went by. It felt so strange because I'd always been passionate about prayer, especially interceding for others. I loved it. Yet in this place of brokenness, I came to an impasse where I didn't know how to pray for my own child much less myself. All out of ideas, I felt drained of faith. *What happened? What do I do with this, Lord? Where do I go from here?* What about you?

Did you question and doubt what you believed about prayer? It's embarrassing to admit, but I had to go back and rework those things. Like some of you, I thought I knew how to pray, but now my prayers felt meager and lacking, empty. Were they really going any farther than the ceiling in my bedroom? On this part of my journey, I made some new discoveries that changed the way I pray. As a result, my prayer life was revitalized. Once again it's become an invaluable lifeline. I'd like to share a few of those discoveries with you.

Use Scripture

On our own, when we've asked God for everything we could think of for our children, seeing no answers, all we can think of is *Help!* After a while we find ourselves saying the same things over and over. A friend showed me a better way by using Bible verses. This was a fresh idea I'd never thought of, despite being a growing Christian for more than thirty-five years. With this approach, you take a passage of Scripture and form it into your own request for your troubled child. Sounds pretty easy, right? It is. After I prayed this way, my soul felt soothed more than usual. I was reading the Bible and praying at the same time. Cool. The Word of God is so powerful that as we use it to pray, we ourselves are able to experience a healing and restoring touch.

For example, take the following scripture: "God is with us; he is our leader. . . . The people . . . were victorious because they relied on the Lord, the God of their ancestors" (2 Chronicles 13:12, 18). Based on that passage, my prayer would be: *Lord, I will rely on You to help me when I'm struggling with fear and worry for Reneé. Instead of trying to cope on my own, I'll lean hard on You, my heavenly guide. Thank You for being with me. I look to You. Lead the way. You're my victory.*

Listen More Than Talk

God intended prayer to be a two-way conversation between us and Him. But when most of us pray—me included—we usually do all the talking, especially when it comes to our troubled child. We think there's a lot we need to tell Him about, even though there isn't anything He's not aware of. Still, we believe we'd better fill Him in, right? I'm really good at that. I turn my prayer into a monologue. I go to great lengths to describe the problem in detail, as though our omniscient God is uninformed. Do you ever do that? And then, after we pour out our complaints, worries, and requests, we think we're done.

What I discovered was that I needed to give Him a chance to respond. Our heavenly Father has things He wants to say to us, too. Imagine that.

It helps to begin by reading some scripture, maybe only a verse or two. Then choose a posture you're comfortable with: sit, kneel, bow, lay face down, or stand. Do whatever is comfortable. There's no right or wrong way. The goal is to be with Him. In your spirit, climb into the lap of God and enjoy some quality time together. Voice your requests and concerns, and then open your heart and receive His love, peace, and calmness. Drink it in.

Next, ask, *God, what do You want to say to me about [your child or one of the issues weighing heavy on your heart]?* Then listen.

Wait patiently with pen and paper in hand. You probably won't hear an audible voice (at least I've never heard one), but in your spirit you may sense a thought. How do you know if it's God speaking and not just your own mind? All I can tell you is that the impressions I get are in alignment with the truths found in the Bible and with God's nature. They're usually not anything I'd ever thought of before. It's always been comforting and enlightening. Be sure to write down what you sense Him saying. You'll want to remember.

One day I was especially upset and worried about Reneé. I decided to have a time of listening prayer with another hurting mom. During that time I received a strong impression of these words, *I've got her.* I believed it was from God, because immediately my heart filled with peace and my anxieties were calmed. It wasn't an assurance she was going to be okay but that He was in control and was with her. How comforting. Years later I've never forgotten.

WRITE OUT YOUR PRAYERS

This doesn't work for everyone, but many find it helpful. Writing out our prayers for our children helps us stay focused and express ourselves differently than when we pray silently. My brain would run off in many different directions: this concern, that fear, the what-ifs, and on it went. The mental gymnastics were exhausting as I tried to keep track of a logical thought. Writing my prayers became a healthy way to stay on track. It also became another way to release my bottled-up emotions. Reading a Bible verse helped me get started, like the example at the beginning of this chapter. Again, when I sensed God speak, I wrote it down and saved it in my journal. When I felt discouraged, I would look back over my entries and find comfort.

BE CONSISTENT

No one else will pray as faithfully for our needy children as we will. That's no big revelation. But I was surprised to realize it was actually possible to think, talk, and worry about Reneé all the time, feeling as though I were praying, but in reality I wasn't. Have you experienced this? I'd describe it more as a running dialogue with God, constantly complaining and fretting. For me, it was better to choose a specific time of day—every morning at 7:00 a.m.—or a certain day of the week when I prayed for her. Many of us pray throughout the day for our children, but choosing a specific time can be helpful.

RECRUIT OTHERS

Another idea is to put together a prayer team. I'd never thought of this before a fellow hurting mom made the suggestion. Ask a few people (as many as you're comfortable with; I started with twelve) to be part of a prayer team for your child. I chose people I knew would be faithful, who really loved and cared about Reneé and my family, who would keep our requests private and confidential, who would take it seriously, and who were strong in their faith.

Explain exactly what you're asking them to do: make a commitment to pray for your child once a week or as often as they'd like. They will pray on their own. You'll e-mail them specific requests and updates once a week and no more, unless there's an emergency. You don't want to overwhelm them. The friends on Reneé's prayer team have told me they appreciated receiving detailed requests because, since they hadn't been in our shoes, they didn't know what to pray for. And they'll want to pray for you too, so be sure to include your personal needs. When answers come, be sure to let them know so they can share in the joys as well as the sorrows.

Having a prayer team was a wonderful blessing that became an invaluable source of support. More than twenty-five dedicated friends—true prayer warriors—have faithfully interceded for Reneé and me for the past ten years. They mean the world to me, and to her too. After Reneé and I reconciled, I told her about them. Today, she sends me requests from time to time and asks that I share them with her prayer team. My, how things can change.

Learn From Others

Take advantage of books about prayer, specifically ones for hurting parents. They were written for this very reason: to help us intercede for our children. There are books for parents of teens, for those with addicted loved ones, for adult children, and for prodigal children in general. Each one I know about was written by a parent who's been there and understands. They wrote from their own experience to support you because they remember what it felt like. When my well ran dry and I didn't know how to pray anymore, I turned to many of these books. I felt like I'd found a gold mine. They were invaluable. There are also prayer websites and Facebook pages. I searched topics like "praying for prodigals" or "praying for your children." See the Resources section at the back of this book for my list under the topic of prayer.

A Warning

To desperate parents eager and willing to do anything to help your child, I need to give a word of caution. We need to be careful not to fall into the trap of thinking there's a magic formula to get God to grant our requests. There isn't one. No foolproof guide exists to receive the answers we want when we want them and in the way we want them. There's no secret verse to claim, no spiritual key you can turn to open your child's heart, no class in seminary or Bible college that teaches these things. But I guarantee you God hears every word you utter in your prayer closet: "One day Jesus told his disciples a story to show that they should always pray and never give up" (Luke 18:1, NLT). He's working where we cannot see. Our job is to persevere, never lose heart, do the best we can in the power of the Holy Spirit, and leave the results in His hands.

Dear friend, remember this: Prayer was never intended to be a way for us to get things *from* God. Prayer was to be our way to be *with* God, to get more of Him. Out of my desperation I'd gotten this turned around and lost perspective. Some of you might have done that too. It's time to reorient our expectations. Come into His presence for more than what you want Him to do for you. When you do, you won't regret it.

I challenge you to choose one idea from this chapter and try it. Pray and keep praying and leave the outcome with God.

Scripture That Helps

Pour out your heart like water in the presence of the Lord. Lift up your hands to him for the lives of your children. (Lamentations 2:19)

15

Surprised by Gratitude

We would worry less if we praised more. Thanksgiving is the enemy of discontent and dissatisfaction.

—H. A. Ironside

Some people don't like surprises. They like knowing what to expect. They're uncomfortable with being caught unawares. Not me. I've always loved surprises, unless it's one of my kids jumping out of a closet to startle me. I've encountered many surprises on my parenting journey. I didn't like many of them, but one of the good ones was what I learned about gratitude.

Does the mere mention of the word *gratitude* make you want to run and hide? When your son or daughter has broken your heart, the last thing you feel like doing is being thankful. I know. You want the world to go away.

But there really is a great deal to be thankful for even when we're in pain because of our children's choices, behaviors, and struggles. When suffering seems to be a way of life, I understand how hard it is to be grateful. It's really easy and natural to get stuck dwelling on the bad things, especially if there are relentless numbers of them. But one thing that helped me get unstuck was when I began to look for something to be grateful for every day, things as simple as sunshine or hearing a bird sing.

Thank You, Lord, I got up today. Thank You, Father, it's not raining. God, I'm thankful that I can see colors and hear music. I started small and let God lead the way from there. Slowly, I chose to develop the habit of gratitude. I didn't feel like it in the beginning—not at all—but in time, being thankful helped me stop feeling sorry for myself. What a surprise to discover the power that had to lift me out of depression. I never would have expected it, but I had to make the choice. Every single day. We need to shift our focus onto positive things instead of always dwelling on the negative our troubled children bring into our world.

DON'T TAKE THIS THE WRONG WAY, BUT . . .

I learned this lesson one day when, feeling more hopeless than usual, full of anxiety, sorrow, and shame, I poured out my complaint to a friend. Things were looking pretty dismal for Reneé. I shared my struggle as honestly as I could.

To my astonishment, my friend paused for a moment and then said, "Dena, please don't be offended or take this the wrong way, but have you been giving thanks? Are you practicing gratitude?"

What? Are you kidding me? No way am I doing that! I wanted to hit him. How in the world could I give thanks? For what? There was nothing to be thankful for. I didn't know if my daughter was dead or alive. How in the world could I be thankful?

"Well, uh, no," I said, restraining my true emotions. "I haven't been doing that. I don't know how. To be honest, I'm not sure I can." I probably had a scowl on my face, though I tried to hide it.

"Dena, I discovered in my own trials with two troubled adult children that gratitude was a key to my well-being. I encourage you to ask God to show you how. He will. I know it seems impossible and it doesn't make any sense when things look so bleak, but I really believe it will make a difference. It could be a long time before you see any changes in your daughter, but this could bring about a change in you. It's worth a try, right?"

Maybe, I thought.

I remembered what the Bible said about gratitude: "Give thanks in all circumstances; for this is God's will for you in Christ Jesus" (1 Thessalonians 5:18). I knew my friend was right, but I still didn't like the idea. I went home and began to wrestle with God. *Lord, I'm so sorry for whining and complaining. You understand. You know all about Reneé. You know my heartache, my feelings of hopelessness, my pity party. I know I'm supposed to give thanks in all conditions. Intellectually I understand that. But this is a tough one. I'm at a loss. It really upsets me even to think about being thankful. In fact, it makes me angry. I haven't even tried. It feels too hard. Besides, wouldn't I be a hypocrite to be thankful when I don't really mean it? You're expecting too much. There's no way. Please help me!*

Over the coming weeks I kept asking God for help. One day, during a time of prayer, I had a breakthrough. I can't explain it. I don't know what happened, but I was able to say, *Okay, Lord, I'm ready. I'm finally willing to be grateful, but You've got to lead the way and do it in me. I need You—a lot. On my own it's impossible. Teach me.*

Slowly, He began to answer my prayers. It would be a choice I had to make, based not on my feelings but on faith, as an act of my will. Like the children's book *The Little Engine That Could,* I'd been telling myself, *I can't.* Now I was saying, *With God, I can.* I started small. "I'm thankful the sky is blue today." "I'm thankful for French vanilla creamer in my decaf." "I'm thankful for air-conditioning in hot, humid weather." "I saw a butterfly." Then I started going deeper, thinking more about Jesus and what He had done for me. Those thoughts drew me to the Cross and all it represented for my life as one of His followers. It pulled me out of my self-centeredness. After all, it was His self-sacrifice that took Him there.

Then I began to think about more that I could be thankful for: my wonderful husband, my other children and family, friends from the past and new ones in the present, amazing counselors, my church community, the privilege of prayer, my home with a pink flowering crepe myrtle tree in the front yard, the ability to see rainbows and sunrises and sunsets, laughter and enjoying funny jokes and good movies, playing games, our sweet dog, fresh fruit, thoughtful gifts from friends, naps on rainy days, my Bible, and the many uplifting books I'd read. Oh yes, and chocolate. Can't forget that. If you give it some effort, I'm sure you can identify a few things you're grateful for too. Why not try right now?[34]

God used gratitude to do a supernatural work in me. He began to knock down the walls of hurt and anger, sadness and despair that I had erected in my heart. Hurt I had harbored toward those who had offended or wounded me and the anger that accompanied it. *I don't deserve to be treated that way. I have every right to be angry. Look what they did to me. How dare they!* Sadness and despair from shattered dreams and a bleak-looking future. *Everything's ruined. What good can come from this? How do I go on from here? Things can't get any worse.* The Father kept whispering, *Give thanks anyway, Dena. Do it no matter how you feel, out of obedience. Look to Me for the strength and courage you need. With Me, you can.*

Today, I'm thankful for so many things. One of the biggest is that Reneé is still alive and doing well despite all the relapses and suicidal times she went through. I'm thankful for the way she tells me she loves me when we talk on the phone and how she gives me a big hug every time I'm with her. I'm thankful our relationship has healed. I'm thankful for our reconciliation. I'm thankful she wants to be with her dad and me and all the family as much as she can. I'm thankful she's discovered the gift of singing, composing, writing, and jewelry making. I'm thankful for all the lives her story has touched. I'm thankful for God's help on my difficult journey. I'm thankful that in the midst of pain and uncertainty, He gives unspeakable peace. I'm thankful that when everything was dark, chaotic, and out of control, God was still in control. His magnificent light broke through and gave me hope. I'm incredibly thankful there is a purpose for our pain. All of it. And I'm thankful that even when I thought my daughter might not live through the night, I knew *I was not alone.*

Heavenly Father, when times are hard, help us shift our focus to choose gratitude instead of grumbling, complaining, or feeling sorry for ourselves. There's always something we can be thankful for. Make us willing to search for it until we find it. Help us give thanks to You, for You are good—all the time—Your love endures forever (Psalm 33:11). You walk by our side through every trial. What comfort this gives. In Your Son's beautiful name. Amen.

Scripture That Helps

The LORD has done great things for us, and we are filled with joy. (Psalm 126:3)

Afterword

The purpose of life is not to be happy—but to matter,
to be productive, to be useful, to have it make some
difference that you have lived at all.

—Leo Rosten

Today, as a result of Reneé's willingness to share her story, the nonprofit To Write Love on Her Arms (TWLOHA.com)[35] came into existence. We had nothing to do with it. Neither did she. It was an amazing, remarkable God thing.

Newspapers, magazines, and *NBC Nightly News* have covered the unique story of the worldwide impact Reneé and TWLOHA have had. In 2009 Reneé published a book, *Purpose for the Pain,* a collection of her journal entries. In 2011 a movie was made about her and the beginnings of the nonprofit. In 2015 Sony Pictures purchased the movie rights. Later that year we attended the premiere, where Reneé sang and spoke, full of grace and wisdom. She's become a singer and songwriter, performing under the stage name Bearcat. Find her on YouTube or iTunes. Look under "Reneé Yohe Bearcat" for video clips.

Out of our own pain, my husband and I started a support group for hurting parents, which eventually turned into a full-time ministry, Hope for Hurting Parents (HHP).[36] Seven years later we're still facilitating groups. Later, we developed a how-to support group facilitator manual, and today we help others start groups all over the country.[37]

Reneé's book, the nonprofit, the movie, and our ministry have been surreal, humbling, exciting, uncomfortable, and wonderful all at the same time. They exist as proof that if we let Him, God can take the worst parts of our lives—our greatest failures, deepest wounds, and most embarrassing moments—and use them for good. He can turn them into something beautiful.

We don't know why these things happened with our story. It's still a mystery. But God works differently in each of us. There may not be a nonprofit, a book, a movie, or a new career for you, but your story will be exactly what He wants it to be. Trust His love and His good plan. You never know what He's preparing for your future.

We've been reconciled to Reneé for over a decade now. Thankfully, the years of destruction have been restored (see Joel 2:25). Our hearts are full of gratitude for what we share with her today.

But you, Mom or Dad, reading these words, what about you? I'm so sorry if you're still in the darkest part of your journey. Restoration could be a long way off or it may never come. You might be in the middle of your worst nightmare, your deepest pit. Your child's story may not have a happy ending. But please hold on to hope.

In spite of what you're going through today or what happens tomorrow, as you embrace these ideas for health and restored relationships, you're going to be okay. As outrageous as it sounds, I agree with William James, who said you can spend your life "for something that will outlast it." How? By what you choose to do with your pain. I urge you to give it to God and allow Him to work out His purpose through it. You can use your brokenness to help someone else. You can be their suitcase carrier. Or you can become someone's prayer warrior and be on their prayer team. You might create inspirational art, write a song or a book, start a blog or a support group or a nonprofit, become an addictions specialist or a counselor or an advocate who promotes mental health issues. Only God knows what it might look like.

Who knows what He could do with your story? The significant thing is for you to surrender, assured that He controls the possibilities. With Him, your life can make a difference. As Reneé likes to say, "Isn't it amazing?"

For Those Who Want to Help Someone Else

Has God given you a burden for hurting parents, even though you aren't one? You may never have walked our path, but you really want to help. Looking at the chapter titles of this book will give you a reminder of some of the issues we deal with every day: disappointment, denial, shock, grief and loss, anger, blame, shame, guilt and embarrassment, fear and worry, feelings of failure and rejection, effects on our marriages or our other children, our health, enabling, powerlessness, exhaustion, despair, and a loss of hope. That's a lot.

How can you help?

- You can walk beside us on our grueling journey while you offer unconditional, Christlike love.

- Simply be there. There's no need for you to have the right words. "I'm sorry" and "I care" are enough.

- Provide heavy doses of TLC, empathy, compassion, patience, and understanding. Encourage us to give ourselves permission to feel our feelings of sadness and loss. Tell us that with God's help we can survive and even thrive again.

- While we struggle with self-blame, embarrassment, and guilt, convince yourself that it's not our fault or we'll be able to sense your disapproval. You could end up doing more harm than good.

- Help us identify the lies of Satan we've believed and replace them with God's truth. You'll hear us voice those false-hoods as you listen to us: "It's my fault." "I should have . . ." "If only . . ." Correct us every chance you get. We need to hear you say it.

- While we grapple with fear and worry, encourage us to be strong and face those things. Help us confront them head on and accept the what-ifs. Don't let us forget that God will be with us no matter what happens, the things we fear may never happen, and we can process our strong emotions about them.

- Gently but strongly push us to keep trusting God no matter how things look, to trust and keep trusting because He loves our child even more than we do.

- Help us avoid being pulled apart from our spouse by persuading us to give special attention to our marriage, to go on a date once a week or every other week and not talk about our troubled offspring, to attend marriage conferences, to seek counseling if needed, and to work hard to be on the same page about our child's issues.

- Encourage us not to isolate and suffer in silence but to talk to safe people. Remind us often that we are not alone and we need to find a support group, such as Al-Anon, Celebrate Recovery, Hope for Hurting Parents, the National Alliance on Mental Illness (NAMI), or some other parent group.

- If our health is suffering, exhort us to please take care of ourselves, get regular exercise and rest, simplify our lives, conserve energy, eat healthy, or see a therapist if we haven't done so yet. Many of us develop all kinds of health problems from our cumulative stress. Tell us to work on one area at a time so we won't get overwhelmed.

- Prod us to give positive attention to our other children since our problem child tends to get most of our focus (even though it's negative). Persuade us to be intentional, to make the effort to spend more quality time together, plan special

outings, compliment and praise them, and show affection
to them.

- When you notice we're being controlling, remind us that
control is an illusion and we need to stop. Help us remember we can't change our child, only God can. We're really
slow to get it.

- Reassure us to keep doing our best while we depend on
God to work.

- Cheer us on to stop enabling and to apply the principles of
tough love: to allow consequences, let our son or daughter
fail early, and not rescue or protect them from natural
outcomes. Those misguided efforts never bring about a
changed heart. Ask us not to deprive our child of the gift
of desperation but instead to let pain do its work.

- Continue to tell us we're doing the right thing when we
detach and let go, when we release our child to God in love,
with hope, to make their own choices and experience the
consequences. Point out that we could actually be getting
in God's way of what He wants to do in their life if we keep
helping. Their trials can have positive benefits.

- When you notice lingering anger or resentment, implore us
to forgive and not let it go on for a long time. Help us see
those things will only hurt us.

Practical Ideas

- Send us frequent e-mails. Don't ask how we're doing.
Instead, ask us how our heart is. Share words of Scripture,
comfort, encouragement, and hope.

- Call us. We feel alone and forgotten. There aren't many
people we can really talk to about this.

- Invite us to meet with you one-on-one and in a private place if possible. This will lessen our embarrassment because we may feel the need to cry. This includes men.
- Offer to pray with us or come to our home and pray there and/or in our child's bedroom, if you're comfortable with this. Many people say they'll pray, but actually praying with us in person is huge.
- Send us Scripture verses on index cards or in text messages.
- Give us simple gifts occasionally: flowers, books, music CDs, an inspirational plaque. Take us out for coffee, dessert, or a meal. It makes us feel special. We really need that.
- Accompany us to a support group meeting if we're reluctant to go by ourselves.
- Offer to sit with us or go with us to the hospital, jail, court, or rehab, especially if we're fearful and have no one who can be with us in an awkward and uncomfortable situation.
- Focus on helping us and not on fixing our child (if only you could). Focus on how we are and what we're feeling.
- Listen more than talk: "Tell me more about that." Practice reflective listening skills to draw us out: "I hear you saying . . ." Ask us good questions: "What are you afraid of?" "What do you think would happen if you stopped . . . ?"
- Be safe and confidential; no gossiping or judging. Give us unconditional acceptance.
- Avoid giving advice. If you do and it turns out you're wrong, we'll blame you. Try to connect us with other hurting parents you may know and with resources in the community.
- Encourage us to take one day at a time, no longer dwelling on the past or looking too far ahead, but focusing on the present.

- Plead with us to strengthen our relationship with Christ. He's our anchor to hold us steady in this storm.
- Be available. Offer companionship and emotional support when needed, but guard your personal boundaries, because we could easily consume too much of your time.
- Encourage us to become informed about our child's issues.
- If our child is under eighteen, urge us to do everything we can to get him or her professional help so we can know we did everything we could. Remind us that we don't want to have any regrets.
- Continually reassure us that we are not alone. We forget. We need your help to remember.

If the Unthinkable Happens

> Death will come to all of us but let us fight
> to live. Let us bury our mothers, for they
> should not bury us.
>
> —Jamie Tworkowski, *If You Feel Too Much*

What if your worst nightmare came true and your child died? It may have been an accidental death, a result of their destructive choices, or by their own hand. If this has happened to you, I'm so sorry. My heart breaks for you to have to endure such a tremendous loss. This section is just for you, for your encouragement and comfort.

These aren't my words. I haven't been where you are. They're heartfelt insights from parents who have experienced the same thing you have. They want to share with you what has helped them and what they wish they'd known. I pray it will be an invaluable resource in the months and years ahead.

FROM A GRIEVING DAD

My wife and I find it helpful to keep in your heart and mind that healing and getting through to the other side of this grief—the deep, deep private pain; the seeming shattering of your very self—may take years. Don't feel like you need to hurry your way through it. You're likely to go around in circles as you slowly inch forward.

Get help when (not if) you need it. Sources of help include the following:

- A pastor or counselor. Ask around since all counselors aren't trained or experienced with grief and loss.

- Communal suffering. It's better than trying to face the deep pain of losing a child alone. Our finding GriefShare—a twelve-week class (GriefShare.org)—was a timely blessed for us. And a local suicide loss survivor's group, as well as our small group at church, were very helpful.
- Books and websites. There are a lot out there. Get advice on what others have found to be the most helpful. Take your time to read and learn and grow. Read a little and think a lot.

Make your family (especially your spouse, if you're married) your ally in suffering. You will need one another more than ever, so avoid isolating yourself with your pain. Lean into each other and force yourself to share your innermost, painful feelings, even if you have to talk in broken sentences through tears. It's better to get the pain out than to act it out in anger and frustration later. Share memories, feelings, and thoughts with each other. Divorce rates for parents who have lost a child are very, very high. Beware that this kind of loss tumbles a marriage into crisis because both your hearts are broken. You can't fix yourself or your spouse.

Keep a journal. Write out your feelings if you can't talk them out.

If you have other children, be prepared to spend extra time with them, but let them grieve in their own way, without pushing them forward. Get them help if they need it, and consider family counseling too. You might even need to encourage your children's friends to rally around them. They may pull away—this can happen to you too—because many haven't faced the pain of losing a family member. They really don't know what your child's going through or how to help.

Pray and talk to God. Ultimately, the pain of this loss, which is so unnatural—children are supposed to outlive their parents and bury them—should drive us to God. He alone understands and draws near to the brokenhearted. Psalms and many promises in the Scriptures offer hope for us and a pathway through our suffering.

From Another Grieving Dad

Try to be a gracious griever. Many people genuinely care but say things they haven't really thought through. They didn't realize how it might make me feel.

For example, a man expressed his condolences about my loss and then went on to tell me about a pastor who had lost his son and used that loss as a platform for sharing Christ. He went on to say how many verses this pastor knew and how impressed he was with this man.

What this man said to me was insensitive. The other father who'd lost his son had nothing to do with my story, thus these comments didn't feel helpful or empathetic. If I were to take his words to heart, I would feel put under the pile that I, too, because I had lost my son, needed to memorize a lot of scripture and use his death as a platform to share the gospel.

With that said though, we do want to trust the Lord to use our story to share God's love and our hope through Jesus Christ. My wife and I have taken several opportunities to do that.

My friend wasn't trying to be insensitive. He was trying to identify with me. He had been inspired by someone else's faith. He didn't mean to hurt me or put pressure on me. In learning to be a gracious griever, when I encounter people like this, I try to listen and then move on.

Similarly, a friend tried to engage me and express empathy, but he pressed too much. In an attempt to connect, he asked a question that brought immediate pain and emotion since it had only been six weeks since my son's death. I excused myself somewhat abruptly. It was important for me to feel the freedom not to answer his question but give myself grace to excuse myself from this friend. Later, I e-mailed him, apologized, and explained why I needed to leave. He expressed understanding and was gracious in return. But it was a very painful experience.

We found Philippians 1:29 to be helpful: "For it has been granted to you on behalf of Christ not only to believe in him, but also to suffer for him." The Philippian church was facing opposition and suffering. We're also enduring great suffering of our hearts and souls. But Paul expressed that this suffering has been granted to us on behalf of Christ, God the Son, by God the Father.

Our suffering has come through the funnel of God's sovereignty and His good plan. I desire to embrace that suffering, just as the Lord suffered, so that I might be granted *to believe in Him.* He has a purpose for our suffering. It will have eternal significance in and through our lives, in the lives of many others, and in His kingdom purposes. This truth gives me hope to continue to walk by faith. It provides a purpose when my *why* questions will never be answered this side of heaven.

FROM A GRIEVING MOM

Every day of my life was recorded in your book.
Every moment was laid out
    before a single day had passed. (Psalm 139:16, NLT)

This verse was my son's Facebook status on January 6. Four and a half months later, this verse was read at his memorial service. When my sister-in-law read it, I was astounded. In the days and weeks that followed, these words became a comfort to me. It was a reminder of God's sovereignty that He knew the exact number of days my son would live on this planet. He knew the day he was born and the day He would take him home.

Be free to feel whatever you're feeling. There's no *right* way to feel after such a devastating loss. You may be numb, angry, or have unstoppable tears at times. I encourage you not to deny your feelings. Healing comes as we don't deny or stuff them.

Try to find at least one or two safe people with whom you can share your feelings or just talk about your child (or scream when you feel the need to). I love any opportunity to talk about my son and share my memories of him.

Let people serve you. Friends and family want to come alongside you. This may be in the form of meals, doing housework, watching children, running errands, helping you make decisions, and so on. It helps them feel good to be able to help and it *is* a help and a blessing. Just receive it.

The biggest encouragement for me during this time has been God's truth and His promises. Most of the time this comes from His Word. If you aren't up for reading, try listening to the Bible on the Internet or listening to praise music. Some great books that have been especially encouraging are *Shattered Dreams: God's Unexpected Path to Joy* by Larry Crabb, *Walking with God Through Pain and Suffering* by Tim Keller (especially parts 2 and 3), *When Your Family's Lost a Loved One: Finding Hope Together* by David and Nancy Guthrie, *In Light of Eternity: Perspectives on Heaven* by Randy Alcorn, *Tear Soup: A Recipe for Healing After Loss* by Pat Schwiebert and Chuck DeKlyen (a children's book with a profound message), and *Experiencing Grief* by H. Norman Wright.

Cry out to the Lord. He is the true source of comfort, even though He's the One who allowed our child to be taken from us. You may be angry at God, and that's okay. I encourage you to talk with someone about that. Since our son died, my husband has written daily in a journal; recording his feelings and what he's learning has been a form of grieving and healing.

Get physical. Even though I wasn't angry at God, I experienced anger at the fact that my son is not with me. At a friend's suggestion, one night my husband and I took a carton of eggs and walked down the street to a wooded area. We cried and one by one, through tears and groaning, threw those eggs at the trees. It was a physical release for me. I'd love to do that with ceramic mugs against a brick wall. I've also found exercise to be helpful. It may be only a walk down the street, but whatever you feel you're able to do, do it.

Try to find a support group for bereaved parents. There's nothing like being able to talk with those who truly understand the devastating pain and struggle of losing a child. If you can't find one right away, there are groups online. One that I found to be encouraging is While We're Waiting, a ministry based in Arkansas. They provide retreats for parents free of charge. They have a closed group on Facebook (While We're Waiting—Support for Bereaved Parents). This is a safe place for us to process our grief with others who are going through the same thing. I've connected with parents whose children have died the same way my son did and whose child died the day after my son did. We share a unique bond, which I would have never chosen, but I'm thankful for it as we walk through this valley together.

When you're able to, praise the Lord. Many times this is an act of worship through tears, and many times it's a sacrifice of praise. But the Lord meets me there. Often my tears flow even more freely at church. There's something about corporate worship and the words of the songs that have taken on a deeper meaning for me now.

The Lord is our anchor and our hope. Our story isn't over, even though it feels like it is. The Lord promises to hold us and carry us as we walk through the valley of the shadow of death. His Word is filled with promises that we can cling to in the midst of our tears and pain. He is a redeemer and He can give us hope as we focus on Him in the midst of our hurt. God promises to use my horrific tragedy for good, and I'm trusting Him to keep that promise.

If the unthinkable happens to you or has already happened, I hope that something in this chapter from an understanding parent will aid you on your journey. "The God of all grace, who called you to his eternal glory in Christ, after you have suffered a little while, will himself restore you and make you strong, firm and steadfast. To him be the power for ever and ever. Amen" (1 Peter 5:10–11).

The Chair Exercise

I talked about this exercise in chapter 3. It was a key to help me process my anger and loss when I became depressed after my miscarriages, and it helped me process my feelings with Reneé years later. Here it is in detail for you if you want to try it.

- Go to a quiet, private place when you have a block of unhurried time.
- Sit in a comfortable chair, both feet on the floor, with another chair across from you or in front of a couch.
- Take a few moments to be still and quiet your thoughts.
- Take three slow, deep, cleansing breaths in through your nose and out through your mouth.
- Imagine God is in the chair across from you. Tell Him everything you've been thinking and feeling and holding in. Say it out loud. Include all your troubling questions. Let your feelings go without censorship. Pound your fist. Stomp your feet. Don't judge yourself. Whatever you need to do is okay.
- When you've let it all out, close your eyes in an attitude of prayer, and ask God what He wants to say back to you.
- Be still. Wait patiently. When intrusive thoughts come to your mind, gently push them aside. Listen closely. Don't be in a hurry.
- Write down what you sense He says, the thoughts and impressions that come to your mind.
- End with a time of gratitude, thanking God for how He spoke to your heart.

More Help for Specific Worries

If your child struggles with a mental illness, I recommend that you attend the National Alliance on Mental Illness (NAMI.org) Family-to-Family course as soon as possible (it's also available online and in Spanish). This free twelve-week educational program is designed to inform, encourage, and empower family members with loved ones who suffer with a mental health problem (also called brain disorders).

Both my husband and I have taken the course and found it exceptionally helpful. At the end of the twelve weeks, we were more aware, understanding, and empathetic with Reneé. Everyone we know who's taken it has had the same outstanding experience, no matter what state they lived in. NAMI also offers family support groups as well as groups for individuals, called Peer-to-Peer. Check out their website to find a group near you.

If you take the class, we encourage you to share what you learn with others. By doing this, we can reduce the stigma and shame historically attached to mental illness. People will be encouraged to be more honest about their struggles and less reticent to seek help. Lives can be saved. NAMI's website is full of helpful information, articles, a monthly newsletter, and more.

If the threat of suicide haunts your home, learn about an effective prevention program called Question-Persuade-Refer (QPR).[38] This simple three-step strategy has been widely successful around the world. Many suicides can be prevented if we learn what to do. It's daunting, but God will supply the courage we lack. We can learn to ask the hard questions even if we're frightened of the answers. He will provide the strength and wisdom we need.

When facing specific worries like these, hold on to this prayer: "For we have no power to face this vast army that is attacking us. We do not know what to do, but our eyes are on you" (2 Chronicles 20:12).

Resources and Book List

General Comfort

Barnes, Emily. *My Cup Overflows . . . with the Comfort of God's Love.* Eugene, OR: Harvest House, 1998.

Coleman, Bill. *Parents with Broken Hearts: Helping Parents of Prodigals to Cope.* Rev. ed. Winona Lake, IN: BMH Books, 2007.

Crabb, Larry. *Shattered Dreams: God's Unexpected Pathway to Joy.* Colorado Springs: WaterBrook, 2001.

Dobson, James. *When God Doesn't Make Sense.* Wheaton, IL: Tyndale, 1993.

Dravecky, Dave. *Do Not Lose Heart: Meditations of Encouragement and Comfort.* Grand Rapids: Zondervan, 2001.

Eldredge, John. *The Journey of Desire: Searching for the Life We've Only Dreamed Of.* Nashville: Thomas Nelson, 2000.

Guthrie, Nancy. *Holding on to Hope: A Pathway Through Suffering to the Heart of God.* Wheaton, IL: Tyndale, 2002.

———. *The One Year Book of Hope.* Wheaton, IL: Tyndale, 2005.

Heatherley, Joyce Landorf. *Balcony People.* Wheaton, IL: Tyndale, 2004.

Hillenbrand, Laura. *Unbroken: A World War II Story of Survival, Resilience, and Redemption.* New York: Random House, 2014.

Keller, Phillip. *A Shepherd Looks at Psalm 23.* Grand Rapids: Zondervan, 1970.

Keller, Timothy. *Walking with God Through Pain and Suffering.* New York: Dutton, 2013.

Kent, Carol. *A New Kind of Normal: Hope-Filled Choices When Life Turns Upside Down.* Nashville: Thomas Nelson, 2007.

———. *When I Lay My Isaac Down: Unshakable Faith in Unthinkable Circumstances.* Colorado Springs: NavPress, 2004.

Lucado, Max. *Fearless: Imagine Your Life Without Fear*. Nashville: Thomas Nelson, 2009.

———. *God Will Use This for Good: Surviving the Mess of Life*. Nashville: Thomas Nelson, 2013.

———. *It's Not About Me: Rescue from the Life We Thought Would Make Us Happy*. Nashville: Integrity, 2004.

Lucas, Jeff. *Will Your Prodigal Come Home? An Honest Discussion of Struggle and Hope*. Grand Rapids: Zondervan, 2007.

Moore, Pamela Rosewell. *Life Lessons from the Hiding Place: Discovering the Heart of Corrie ten Boom*. Grand Rapids: Chosen, 2004.

Morgan, Robert J. *Moments for Families with Prodigals*. Colorado Springs: NavPress, 2003.

O'Rourke, Brendan, and DeEtte Sauer. *The Hope of a Homecoming: Entrusting Your Prodigal to a Sovereign God*. Colorado Springs: NavPress, 2003.

Tada, Joni Eareckson. *Joni: An Unforgettable Story*. 25th anniversary ed. Grand Rapids: Zondervan, 2001.

———. *A Place of Healing: Wrestling with the Mysteries of Suffering, Pain, and God's Sovereignty*. Colorado Springs: David C. Cook, 2010.

Thompson, Marjorie J., and Stephen D. Bryant. *Companions in Christ: The Way of Forgiveness: Participant's Book*. Nashville: Upper Room, 2002.

Tworkowski, Jamie. *If You Feel Too Much: Thoughts on Things Found and Lost and Hoped For*. New York: Jeremy P. Tarcher, 2015.

Voskamp, Ann. *One Thousand Gifts: A Dare to Live Fully Right Where You Are*. Grand Rapids: Zondervan, 2010.

Vujicic, Nick. *Life Without Limits: Inspiration for a Ridiculously Good Life*. Colorado Springs: WaterBrook, 2010.

Walsh, Sheila. *Life Is Tough but God Is Faithful*. Nashville: Thomas Nelson, 1999.

Warren, Rick. *The Purpose-Driven Life: What on Earth Am I Here For?* Grand Rapids: Zondervan, 2002.

Welch, Reuben. *We Really Do Need Each Other.* Nashville: Impact Books, 1982.

Wright, H. Norman. *Experiencing Grief.* Nashville: B&H Publishing Group, 2004.

———. *Loving a Prodigal: A Survival Guide for Parents of Rebellious Children.* Colorado Springs: Chariot Victor, 1999.

Yancey, Philip. *Disappointment with God: Three Questions No One Asks Aloud.* New York: HarperCollins, 1988.

Yohe, Reneé. *Purpose for the Pain.* Orlando, FL: Bonded Books, 2008.

Zamperini, Louis, and David Rensin. *Don't Give Up, Don't Give In: Lessons from an Extraordinary Life.* New York: HarperCollins, 2014.

Prayer

Banks, James. *Prayers for Prodigals: 90 Days of Prayer for Your Child.* Grand Rapids: RBC Ministries, 2011.

Berndt, Jodie. *Praying the Scriptures for Your Teenagers: Discover How to Pray God's Will for Their Lives.* Grand Rapids: Zondervan, 2007.

Cosby, Sharron. *Praying for Your Addicted Loved One: 90 in 90.* Auburn, WA: Bookjolt, 2013.

Logan, Jim. *Reclaiming Surrendered Ground: Protecting Your Family from Spiritual Attacks.* Chicago: Moody, 1995.

Lucas, Jeff. *Will Your Prodigal Come Home? An Honest Discussion of Struggle and Hope.* Grand Rapids: Zondervan, 2007.

Morgan, Robert J. *Moments for Families with Prodigals.* Colorado Springs: NavPress, 2003.

Omartian, Stormie. *The Power of a Praying Parent.* Eugene, OR: Harvest House, 2014.

———. *The Power of Praying for Your Adult Children.* Eugene, OR: Harvest House, 2009.

Roberts, Lee. *Praying God's Will for My Daughter.* Rev. ed. Nashville: Thomas Nelson, 2002.

———. *Praying God's Will for My Son.* Rev. ed. Nashville: Thomas Nelson, 2002.

Thompson, Janet. *Praying for Your Prodigal Daughter: Hope, Help and Encouragement for Hurting Parents.* New York: Howard Books, 2007.

Websites:

Breakthrough, www.intercessors.org.

Facebook pages: 365 Days of Prayers for Prodigals; Prayer for Prodigals; The Prodigal Hope Network.

Prayer for Prodigals, http://prayerforprodigals.com, developed by Cru (formerly Campus Crusade for Christ). Request an invitation via e-mail: prayerforprodigals@gmail.com. This is a password-protected site on which you can post prayer requests and receive prayers back from participants by e-mail. It's full of resources: Scripture verses, prayers, recommended books, inspirational devotionals, and places for help around the country for many issues (therapeutic boarding schools for teens, drug and alcohol rehabs, wilderness camps for youth, eating disorder programs, and more).

Addiction

Alcoholics Anonymous. *The Big Book.* 4th ed. New York: Alcoholics Anonymous World Services, 2001. Available at meetings and online. Brochures are available at meetings.

Alcoholics Anonymous. *Courage to Change: One Day at a Time in Al-Anon II.* New York: Alcoholics Anonymous World Services, 1992. Available at meetings and online. Brochures are available at meetings.

Conyers, Beverly. *Addict in the Family: Stories of Loss, Hope, and Recovery.* Center City, MN: Hazelden, 2003.

———. *Everything Changes: Help for Families of Newly Recovering Addicts.* Center City, MN: Hazelden, 2009.

Hayden, Karilee, and Wendi Hayden English. *Wild Child, Waiting Mom: Finding Hope in the Midst of Heartache.* Wheaton, IL: Tyndale, 2006.

Hersh, Sharon. *The Last Addiction: Why Self-Help Is Not Enough, Own Your Desire, Live Beyond Recovery, Find Lasting Freedom.* Colorado Springs: WaterBrook, 2008.

Lawford, Kennedy. *Moments of Clarity: Voices from the Front Lines of Addiction and Recovery.* New York: HarperCollins, 2009.

VanVonderen, Jeff. *Hope and Help for the Addicted.* Grand Rapids: Revell, 2004.

Vawter, John, ed. *Hit by a Ton of Bricks.* Little Rock, AR: Family Life Publishing, 2003.

White, John. *Parents in Pain: A Book of Comfort and Counsel.* Downers Grove, IL: InterVarsity, 1979.

Websites:

About Alcoholism, www.aboutalcoholism.org.

Al-Anon Family Groups, www.al-anon.org.

Celebrate Recovery, www.celebraterecovery.com.

Co-Dependents Anonymous, www.coda.org.

Nar-Anon Family Groups, www.nar-anon.org.

Boundaries

Adams, Jane. *When Our Grown Kids Disappoint Us: Letting Go of Their Problems, Loving Them Anyway, and Getting On with Our Lives.* New York: Free Press, 2003.

Beattie, Melodie. *Codependent No More: How to Stop Controlling Others and Start Caring for Yourself.* Center City, MN: Hazelden, 1992.

Bottke, Allison. *Setting Boundaries with Your Adult Children*. Eugene, OR: Harvest House, 2008.

Cloud, Henry, and John Townsend. *Boundaries: When to Say Yes, When to Say No to Take Control of Your Life*. Grand Rapids: Zondervan, 1992.

Friends in Recovery. *The Twelve Steps for Christians from Addictive and Other Dysfunctional Families: Based on Biblical Teachings*. San Diego: Recovery Publications, 1988.

Rubin, Charles. *Don't Let Your Kids Kill You: A Survival Guide for Parents of Drug Addicts and Alcoholics*. 3rd ed. Petaluma, CA: NewCentury, 2010.

For Parents of Troubled Adolescents

Dobson, James. *The New Strong-Willed Child: Birth Through Adolescence*. Wheaton, IL: Tyndale, 2004.

Gregston, Mark. *When Your Teen Is Struggling*. Eugene, OR: Harvest House, 2007. See also the website www.heartlightministries.org.

Hersh, Sharon. *Mom, Everyone Else Does! Becoming Your Daughter's Ally in Responding to Peer Pressure to Drink, Smoke, and Use Drugs*. Colorado Springs: WaterBrook, 2005.

———. *Mom, I Feel Fat! Becoming Your Daughter's Ally in Developing a Healthy Body Image*. Colorado Springs: Shaw, 2001.

———. *Mom, I Hate My Life: Becoming Your Daughter's Ally Through the Emotional Ups and Downs of Adolescence*. Colorado Springs: WaterBrook, 2004.

———. *Mom, Sex Is No Big Deal! Becoming Your Daughter's Ally in Developing a Healthy Sexual Identity*. Colorado Springs: Shaw, 2006.

Jantz, Gregory L. *When Your Teenager Becomes the Stranger in Your House*. Colorado Springs: David C. Cook, 2011.

Scott, Buddy. *Relief for Hurting Parents: What to Do and How to Think When You're Having Trouble with Your Kids*. Nashville:

Oliver-Nelson, 1989. See also the author's website: www.buddyscott
.com.

Tripp, Paul David. *Age of Opportunity: A Biblical Guide to Parenting
Teens.* Phillipsburg, NJ: P&R Publishing, 1997, 2001. See also the
author's website: www.paultripp.com.

Website: Dr. James Dobson's Family Talk, http://drjamesdobson.org.

Bullying

Bullying in a Cyber World, Grades 4 to 5. Rowley, MA: Didax, 2012.
Additional materials are available for parents and schools.

Bullying in a Cyber World, Grades 6 to 8. Rowley, MA: Didax, 2012.
Additional materials are available for parents and schools.

Gerali, Steve. *What Do I Do When Teenagers Encounter Bullying and
Violence?* Grand Rapids: Zondervan, 2009.

Mayo Clinic Staff. "Bullying: Help Your Child Handle a Bully." August
23, 2013. www.mayoclinic.org/healthy-living/childrens-health
/in-depth/bullying/art-20044918?pg=1.

Miller, Cindy, and Cynthia Lowen. *The Essential Guide to Bullying
Prevention and Intervention: Protecting Children and Teens from
Physical, Emotional, and Online Bullying.* New York: Alpha
Books, 2012.

National Education Association. *Bully Free: It Starts with Me.* The
National Education Association (NEA; www.nea.org) program to
stop bullying in public schools.

Students Against Being Bullied, SABB Inc., www.studentsagainst
beingbullied.org, offers antibullying programs that can be used in
schools.

van der Zande, Irene. "Face Bullying with Confidence: 8 Kidpower
Skills We Can Use Right Away." Santa Cruz, CA: Kidpower,
2011.

———. *Kidpower Solutions.* Santa Cruz, CA: Kidpower, 2010.

Mental Health

Alcorn, Nancy. *Starved: Mercy for Eating Disorders*. Enumclaw, WA: Winepress, 2007.

Amador, Xavier. *I Am Not Sick, I Don't Need Help: How to Help Someone with Mental Illness Accept Treatment*. Peconic, NY: Vida Press, 2010. See also the website www.leapinstitute.org.

Duke, Patty, and Gloria Hochman. *A Brilliant Madness: Living with Manic-Depressive Illness*. New York: Bantam, 1992.

Evans, Dwight L., and Linda Wasmer Andrews. *If Your Adolescent Has Depression or Bipolar Disorder: An Essential Resource for Parents*. New York: Oxford University Press, 2006.

Federman, Russ, and J. Anderson Thomson. *Facing Bipolar: The Young Adult's Guide to Dealing with Bipolar Disorder*. Oakland, CA: New Harbinger, 2010.

Hornbacher, Marya. *Wasted: A Memoir of Anorexia and Bulimia*. New York: HarperCollins, 1999.

Jamison, Kay Redfield. *An Unquiet Mind*. New York: Knopf, 1995.

Levine, Jerome, and Irene S. Levine. *Schizophrenia for Dummies*. Hoboken, NJ: Wiley, 2009.

Mason, Paul T., and Randi Kreger. *Stop Walking on Eggshells: Taking Your Life Back When Someone You Care About Has Borderline Personality Disorder*. Oakland, CA: New Harbinger, 2010.

Mondimore, Francis M. *Bipolar Disorder: A Guide for Patients and Families*. Baltimore: Johns Hopkins University Press, 1999.

Morrow, Jena. *Hope for the Hollow: A Thirty-Day Inside-Out Makeover for Women Recovering from Eating Disorders*. Raleigh, NC: Lighthouse Publishing, 2013.

Mueser, Kim T., and Susan Gingerich. *The Complete Family Guide to Schizophrenia: Helping Your Loved One Get the Most out of Life*. New York: Guilford, 2006.

Walsh, Sheila. *Loved Back to Life: How I Found the Courage to Live Free.* Nashville: Thomas Nelson, 2015.

Zayfert, Claudia, and Jason C. DeViva. *When Someone You Love Suffers from Posttraumatic Stress: What to Expect and What You Can Do.* New York: Guilford, 2011.

Websites:
　　Bring Change 2 Mind, www.bringchange2mind.org.
　　International Bipolar Foundation (IBPF), http://ibpf.org.
　　National Alliance on Mental Illness (NAMI), www.nami.org.
　　To find a counselor: www.findchristiancounselor.com or www.psychologytoday.com.

Self-Injury (Self-Harm, Self-Mutilation)

Alcorn, Nancy. *Cut.* Enumclaw, WA: Winepress, 2007.

Leatham, Victoria. *Bloodletting: A Memoir of Secrets, Self-Harm, and Survival.* Oakland, CA: New Harbinger, 2006.

Strong, Marilee. *A Bright Red Scream: Self-Mutilation and the Language of Pain.* New York: Viking, 1998.

Websites:
　　The Butterfly Project, www.butterfly-project.tumblr.com.
　　Mercy Multiplied, http://mercymultiplied.com.
　　SAFE Alternatives (Self Abuse Finally Ends), www.selfinjury.com; information hotline: 800-DONTCUT (366-8288).
　　Self-Mutilators Anonymous (SMA), www.selfmutilatorsanonymous.org.

Same-Sex Attraction

Dallas, Joe. *The Gay Gospel? How Pro-Gay Advocates Misread the Bible.* Eugene, OR: Harvest House, 2007.

———. *When Homosexuality Hits Home: What to Do When a Loved One Says They're Gay.* Eugene, OR: Harvest House, 2004.

Haley, Mike. *101 Frequently Asked Questions About Homosexuality.*
Eugene, OR: Harvest House, 2004.

Johnson, Barbara. *When Your Child Breaks Your Heart: Help for Hurting Moms.* Grand Rapids: Baker Publishing, 1979.

Kaltenbach, Caleb. *Messy Grace: How a Pastor with Gay Parents Learned to Love Others Without Sacrificing Conviction.* Colorado Springs: WaterBrook, 2015.

Martin, Andrew. *Love Is an Orientation: Elevating the Conversation with the Gay Community.* Downers Grove, IL: InterVarsity, 2009.

Worthen, Anita, and Bob Davies. *Someone I Love Is Gay: How Family and Friends Can Respond.* Downers Grove, IL: InterVarsity, 1996.

Website: Living Hope, www.livehope.org.

Sensory Processing Disorder

Heller, Sharon. *Too Loud, Too Bright, Too Fast, Too Tight: What to Do If You Are Sensory Defensive in an Overstimulating World.* New York: HarperCollins, 2002. See also the author's website: www.sharonheller.net.

Kranowitz, Carol. *The Out-of-Sync Child: Recognizing and Coping with Sensory Processing Disorder.* New York: Penguin, 2005. See also the STAR Center: Sensory Therapies and Research website: www.spdstar.org.

Sexual Abuse

Haughton, Debbie. "What Is EMDR and Can It Help My Child?" *Hope for Hurting Parents* (blog). http://hopeforhurtingparents .wordpress.com/2014/06/18/what-is-emdr-and-can-it-help-my -child.

The Healing Tree. Orange Country, FL. http://caccentral.com/the -healing-tree. Search online for sexual assault programs in your county or city to find help for yourself or your child.

Heitritter, Lynn, and Jeanette Vough. *Helping Victims of Sexual Abuse.* Minneapolis: Bethany, 2006.

Mann, Mary Ellen. *From Pain to Power: Overcoming Sexual Trauma and Reclaiming Your True Identity.* Colorado Springs: Water-Brook, 2015.

Oakley, Diana. *Intended Harm.* Orlando, FL: Legacy Publishing, 2012.

O'Branyll, Fiona. *A Bright New Place: Triumph After Trauma.* Bloomington, IN: Westbow, 2013.

Omartian, Stormie. *Just Enough Light for the Step I'm On.* Eugene, OR: Harvest House, 1999.

Websites:

Restoring the Heart Ministries (www.rthm.cc). See *In the Wild-flowers,* support group material written by Julie Woodley, a ten-part DVD series focused on recovery from sexual trauma. It was produced in cooperation with the American Association of Christian Counselors (www.aacc.net). Call 1-800-526-8673 for more information.

Victim Service Centers: Search online to find one in your county or for sexual assault hotlines.

Suicide

Biebel, David B., and Suzanne L. Foster. *Finding Your Way After the Suicide of Someone You Love.* Grand Rapids: Zondervan, 2005.

Fine, Carla. *No Time to Say Goodbye: Surviving the Suicide of a Loved One.* New York: Doubleday, 1997.

Hope for the Heart: 1-800-488-4673 (HOPE). Website: www.hope fortheheart.org.

The Hope Line: 1-800-394-4673 (HOPE). Coaches are available 24/7. Website: www.thehopeline.com.

Hsu, Albert Y. *Grieving a Suicide: A Loved One's Search for Comfort, Answers, and Hope.* Downers Grove, IL: InterVarsity, 2002.

Jamison, Kay Redfield. *Night Falls Fast: Understanding Suicide.* New York: Knopf, 1999.

National Suicide Prevention Lifeline: 1-800-273-8255 (TALK). Call 24/7, 365 days a year, including holidays. Website: www.suicide preventionlifeline.org.

QPR Institute, suicide prevention training. Free e-book, *Suicide: The Forever Decision.* Website: www.qprinstitute.com.

Smolin, Ann, and John Guinan. *Healing After the Suicide of a Loved One.* New York: Simon & Schuster, 1993.

Websites:

American Foundation of Suicide Prevention, www.afsp.org.

Survivors of Suicide, www.survivorsofsuicide.com. Offers links to find support groups.

Acknowledgments

Thank you, Reneé, my precious princess, for giving your blessing to write this book with authenticity and for the hours of soul-searching you did for your comments. Those insights will be invaluable to many parents. God bless you for your courage. Your dad and I are so proud of you. Because you were willing to share your private pain-filled story, people around the world have found the help and hope they needed. They came to believe they were not alone. How extraordinary! You'll never know how much you've inspired us and countless others. You're making a difference that will outlast you. Isn't it amazing?

Thank you, Michael and April, my oldest and youngest, and your spouses, Becky and Nick, for your support, your belief in me, and your undying love for your sister. Compassionate, understanding, and forgiving, you're beautiful grace givers. I'm proud to call you family.

Thank you, my dear friends and stretcher bearers, who journeyed with me and challenged me to write this book. You've been a steady source of encouragement, wisdom, gentle prodding, and constant prayer: Karen Akers, Terri Amos, Polly Anthony, Debbi DeCola, Anne Fallow, Judy Douglass, Suzanne Howe, Evelyn Lechliter, Gail Porter, Dayle Rogers, Barb Whitehouse, my fellow writers at Word Weavers (Orlando Chapter), and too many others to name. I could never have done this without you.

Tom and I also want to thank the many heroes God brought along the way. Ryan Kirkland, you were a significant one. Each person was most unexpected. You showed up at the right places and the right times in Reneé's life and in ours. Our daughter might not be alive today if not for some of you. The way you gave of yourselves out of Christlike love and genuine concern, expecting nothing in return, was astounding. You lavished us with love, encouragement, comfort, strength, patience, acceptance, friendship, and, when ours was gone, hope. Through you, we learned deep lessons of gratitude in the midst of our suffering.

One of you knelt on the floor in front of me as you prayed, while your tears dripped on my feet, ministering deep comfort to my grief-stricken heart.

Another said, "Dena, I'll hold on to hope for you until yours returns."

Another cleaned blood from a car and the sidewalk nearby after a brutal incident of Reneé's self-directed violence when all I could do was sit and bawl, incapacitated. She wept, too, as she washed and prayed. What a sacrificial gift of love.

Then there was the stranger who happened to be in a public restroom at the exact moment I ran into it, looking for a private place to break down. She held me, cried with me, and prayed for me. It turned out that she, too, was on her own difficult parenting journey. I felt as though I'd been with an angel.

Special thanks to Amanda Luedeke, my agent at MacGregor Literary, who believed in me. Without you, this book would not have become a reality.

And I thank God, who helped me survive, come to thrive again, gave me the dream of this book, and then gave me the courage to write it.

A Tribute to David

One of my heroes on our journey is David McKenna. He was one of the people God used to show us that He was working where we couldn't. The ways He worked through this young man gave us hope when we were losing ours. Our lives converged over a period of eight years. Tom and I came to love David like a son because of his sincere heart to help Reneé and his thoughtfulness toward us. An ex-cocaine addict, he had been delivered and reborn in Christ. You can watch a video of him sharing his story on the I Am Second website (www.iamsecond.com/seconds /david-mckenna).

If you watch the interview, you'll see that David was a passionate, winsome gentleman with a Cheshire-cat smile. Muscular, tan, well-groomed, and fashionably dressed, he commanded attention when he entered a room. With his dynamic personality, it's understandable how he and Reneé quickly formed a deep connection. They met the night before she headed off to rehab the first time. In that life-changing encounter, David made Reneé a promise to be there for her when she returned, to show her how to live a sober life, and to help her build a supportive community.

He kept his promise. And he came to love her and feel protective of her like a big brother. She felt the same way about him.

During each of her relapses, David stayed in touch with Reneé as much as possible. He had to be careful, though, not to jeopardize his own recovery. But without fail, he always accepted her and loved her just as she was, without judgment or lectures.

Since he had been in her shoes, he had a sixth sense about addiction. He could tell when she wasn't doing well, yet he never gave up on her, never stopped being a true friend, never stopped reaching out to her, and never refused her desperate 2:00 a.m. phone calls, knowing her life could be in danger—again. He was determined to make a difference in her life.

The reason David had such a huge impact on Reneé was because of the trusting relationship he built with her. When he and his friends dared to care enough to put their love into action, it turned into something more than anyone could have imagined. In Reneé's words:

> Thank you for speaking into my life. Thank you for restoring my faith in humanity. Thank you for being a warrior on my behalf, a man of action and wisdom. Thank you for being the vessel that God used to give me a second chance at life. Through your transparency God spoke to me that night and started me on the first steps toward recovery. Then He brought you back into my life with a community and a love more powerful than I had ever known, and you had the strength to hurt with me as I banged my head again and again in addiction. You let me flail until I wanted help, and when that moment came, you were there to fight the world for my life. I will be forever grateful for you, what you have done for me, who you are to me now, my dear, dear friend, and the role you have in my future.[39]

Because of David's entrepreneurial and visionary nature, three years into Reneé's recovery, he urged her to publish the book that became *Purpose for the Pain*,[40] a collection of her poetic journal entries. And a year after that he spearheaded and coproduced the movie *To Write Love on Her Arms*. Why? To bring hope to still more people who struggled with the same issues she did. You can learn more about the movie or watch it by doing an online search and checking most online media sources. It's also available to purchase from TWLOHA.com in their store under Accessories.

Our thirty-year-old hero endeared himself to our hearts by the way he constantly showed us compassion. When David knew Reneé was in a bad way, he'd call us to ask how we were doing, taking time out of an already packed schedule to meet for coffee, just to encourage us. His caring, empathetic voice was the one we'd hear on the other end of the phone in the middle of the night every time Reneé ended up in the hospital. She would call David. He would go to her to help. Then he would call us.

"Tom, it's David. I'm so sorry to call you at this hour, but I need to let you know about Reneé . . ."

As we got to know him, David explained how much agony he knew he'd put his own parents through. It hurt him deeply to realize the suffering he'd caused them. Experiencing their pain up close and personal through our eyes put it all in a whole new light. One day he confided those feelings:

> My parents were wonderful, the best. They didn't do anything
> to deserve what they got from me. I don't fault them at all. I was
> bullheaded and stubborn. I thought I knew better. I feel abso-
> lutely terrible now to think about what I did to them, especially
> my mother. It's one of the reasons I empathize so much with the
> two of you. If I can help you at all, it's one way for me to make
> amends for how much I hurt my own family.

God bless you, David. Your parents are so proud of the man you've become.

That experience created in him a special tenderness toward us. He reached out regularly to offer comfort and a listening ear. And he would open up about his own struggles. He had his share of relapses too, but he was always honest about them. During those times we had the privilege of being able to encourage him. He grew to have a special place in our hearts.

Sometimes he'd call and say, "Hey, Tom, it's been too long, man.

There are some things going on in my life that I'd love to talk with you about. Are you free this afternoon?"

On December 14, 2012, we received the shocking news that David had been killed in a car accident. Words cannot express our sorrow over this loss. He had become Reneé's closest, most trusted friend, ally, and mentor. He made a huge difference in her life. David believed in her, and he believed in us. God used him to help her dream big dreams, and He used him to make some of them come true.

David, we'll be forever thankful to God for you. You'll always be one of our heroes.

A friend encouraged me with these words one day (before we met David), when I was wondering where God was and what He was doing: "When you can't trace God's hand, trust His heart." That's what He wants us to do. Trust His heart. There's no guarantee you'll get a David. He doesn't work the same way in everyone's life. He's much bigger than that. But you can depend on Him, Mom or Dad. God's ways are far better than ours. Far better.

"'For my thoughts are not your thoughts, neither are your ways my ways,' declares the LORD. 'As the heavens are higher than the earth, so are my ways higher than your ways and my thoughts than your thoughts'" (Isaiah 55:8–9).

Notes

1. In chapter 12, I'll address the answers I found. They're important to answer when life disappoints us. The wrong answers can derail our faith, encourage us to believe lies, and lead to faulty beliefs.
2. See www.sheknows.com/baby-names/search/renee and www .behindthename.com/name/rene10e/comments: "reborn." See also Free Dictionary, http://encyclopedia.thefreedictionary.com /Renee.
3. Quoted in Tom Yohe and Dena Yohe, "Parents: Learn About Self-Injury from a Counselor," Hope for Hurting Parents, May 29, 2014, www.hopeforhurtingparents.com/?p=1922.
4. Sharon Heller, *Too Loud, Too Bright, Too Fast, Too Tight: What to Do If You Are Sensory Defensive in an Overstimulating World* (New York: HarperCollins, 2002), 3.
5. Charles Rubin, *Don't Let Your Kids Kill You: A Guide for Parents of Drug and Alcohol Addicted Children,* 3rd ed. (1996; Petaluma, CA: NewCentury, 2010), 2.
6. A great deal of assistance is available for parents and children on bullying. We can inform ourselves and teach our kids how to handle the situation. We can go a step further and encourage their school to take action. See the Resources and Book List in this book for some excellent resources.
7. Melinda Smith and Jeanne Segal, "Cutting and Self-Harm: Self-Injury Help, Support, and Treatment," HelpGuide.org, September 2015, www.helpguide.org/articles/anxiety/cutting-and -self-harm.htm. For this section on self-injury, see also Reneé Yohe, *Purpose for the Pain* (Orlando, FL: Bonded Books, 2009), November 17, 2003.

8. See the bullying resources in the Resources and Book List in this book to learn what your options are. You may want to encourage your school to adopt an antibullying campaign.

9. Kay Redfield Jamison, *Night Falls Fast: Understanding Suicide* (New York: Random House, 1999), 95.

10. See the Resources and Book List in this book for published and online information available for parents of troubled adolescents.

11. I found prayer warriors through my church and friends. If your church doesn't offer this, call some churches in your area and inquire if they have a prayer ministry to people in the community. An online resource is Hope for the Heart (www.hopefortheheart. org), which can offer a care team to talk with you 24/7.

12. M. Scott Peck, *Further Along the Road Less Traveled: The Unending Journey Toward Spiritual Growth: The Edited Lectures* (New York: Simon & Schuster, 1993), 46.

13. Quoted in "Inspirational Readings on Forgiveness: Day 18 of 40: The Difference Between Excusing and Forgiving," Explore God, www.exploregod.com/40-inspirational-readings-on-forgiveness /the-difference-between-excusing-and-forgiving.

14. My friend quoted Louis B. Smedes, *The Art of Forgiving* (New York: Random House, 1996), 178.

15. Allison Bottke, *Setting Boundaries with Your Adult Children: Six Steps to Hope and Healing for Struggling Parents* (Eugene, OR: Harvest House, 2008), 92.

16. Bottke, *Setting Boundaries,* 44.

17. Suggested books include Bottke, *Setting Boundaries,* and Henry Cloud and John Townsend, *Boundaries: When to Say Yes, How to Say No to Take Control of Your Life* (Grand Rapids: Zondervan, 1992).

18. From an interview with Brené Brown posted on the Work of the People Facebook site, March 5, 2016.

19. Charles R. Swindoll, *The Grace Awakening* (Dallas: Word, 1990), 146–47.

20. "Resilience: Failure, Rejection, Grit," *Psychology Today*, www .psychologytoday.com/basics/resilience.

21. H. Norman Wright, *Experiencing Grief* (Nashville: B&H Group, 2002), 53.

22. Quoted at "Mundane Faithfulness: Kara Tippetts Finishes," Summit Ministries, March 25, 2015, http://summit.org/blogs /summit-announcements/mundane-faithfulness-kara-tippetts -finishes-.

23. H. Norman Wright, *Surviving a Prodigal* (Colorado Springs: Chariot Victor, 1999), 227.

24. Thelma Thompson, quoted in Dale Carnegie, *How to Stop Worrying and Start Living* (New York: Pocket Books, 1984), 139.

25. Jamie Tworkowski, "To Write Love on Her Arms," To Write Love on Her Arms, http://twloha.com/learn/story.

26. James Dobson, *When God Doesn't Make Sense* (Wheaton, IL: Tyndale, 1993), 236–37.

27. Dobson, *When God Doesn't Make Sense,* 238.

28. Max Lucado, *It's Not About Me: Rescue from the Life We Thought Would Make Us Happy* (Nashville: Thomas Nelson, 2011), 121–22.

29. See www.geocaching.com. Wikipedia describes geocaching as "an outdoor recreational activity, in which participants use a GPS . . . to hide and seek containers, called 'geocaches' or 'caches,' anywhere in the world."

30. Kara Tippetts, *The Hardest Peace: Expecting Grace in the Midst of Life's Hard* (Colorado Springs: David C. Cook, 2014), 71.

31. See Kara Tippetts's website: www.mundanefaithfulness.com.

32. Carol Kent, *A New Kind of Normal: Hope-Filled Choices When Life Turns Upside Down* (Nashville: Thomas Nelson, 2007), dedication page.

33. Lucado, *It's Not About Me,* 126.

34. A favorite book on the topic of gratitude is Ann Voskamp, *One Thousand Gifts: A Dare to Live Fully Right Where You Are* (Grand Rapids: Zondervan, 2010). I urge you to read it and also check out her Facebook page: Ann Voskamp.

35. To Write Love on Her Arms (www.twloha.org) is a nonprofit movement dedicated to presenting hope and finding help for people struggling with depression, addiction, self-injury, and suicide. TWLOHA exists to encourage, inform, inspire, and invest directly in treatment and recovery.

36. See www.hopeforhurtingparents.com and its Facebook page: Hope for Hurting Parents.

37. HHP facilitator manual topics include grief and loss, guilt, worry and anxiety, fear, detachment, anger, letting go, enabling, powerlessness, hope, and self-care. They can be requested by contacting us through the website www.hopeforhurtingparents.com. We also offer personal mentoring for facilitators. These support groups are confidential, loving communities where parents can find the encouragement, resources, acceptance, comfort, and hope they need.

38. QPR Institute for Suicide Prevention: www.qprinstitute.com.

39. Renée Yohe, *Purpose for the Pain* (Orlando, FL: Bonded, 2009), acknowledgments.

40. Renée's book *Purpose for the Pain* is available from the TWLOHA online store, http://store.twloha.com/products/purpose-for-the -pain-book.